ALTERNATIVES TO THE MULTINATIONAL ENTERPRISE

ALTERNATIVES TO THE MULTINATIONAL ENTERPRISE

Mark Casson

HOLMES & MEIER PUBLISHERS, INC.
IMPORT DIVISION
30 Irving Place, New York, N.Y. 10003

First published 1979 by
THE MACMILLAN PRESS LTD
London and Basingstoke
Associated companies in Delhi
Dublin Hong Kong Johannesburg Lagos
Melbourne New York Singapore Tokyo

Typeset by
Preface Ltd
Salisbury, Wilts.
and printed in Great Britain by
Billing & Sons Limited
Guildford, London and Worcester

British Library Cataloguing in Publication Data

Casson, Mark
    Alternatives to the multinational enterprise
    1. Technology transfer   2. International
    business enterprises   3. Investments, Foreign
    4. Capital investments
    I. Title
    338.4'5   T174.3

    ISBN 0–333–26447–9

For Joyce, my mother-in-law

Contents

THEORY

Introduction

In the postwar world the main role of the multinational enterprise has been the international diffusion of proprietary technology and managerial skills. Whether host countries always need advanced technology to service domestic consumption is debatable, but such technology is usually indispensable if host countries are to remain competitive in manufacturing exports.

However, by using foreign direct investment as the instrument of technology transfer the multinational firm has not only retained exclusive control of its own technology but acquired control over investment and employment decisions in host countries. Wherever foreign direct investment is a significant proportion of total manufacturing investment – e.g. in less developed countries on the periphery of the developed world – problems have arisen in reconciling the objectives of the firm with those of the host government. Host governments, therefore, seek ways of importing technology without surrendering control of investment and employment decisions in key sectors of their economies. This can be achieved either by restricting the operations of firms by statutory regulations, or by seeking alternative institutional arrangements for the transfer of technology. This book is motivated by a belief that it is the second approach which is the most promising. One of its objectives is to evaluate an arrangement for separating control of the development of a technology from control of production processes exploiting that technology. Such separation must harmonise the interests of the proprietor of the technology and of the host country through a negotiated contractual arrangement. We therefore argue that changing host country attitudes are making it opportune to revive the concept of an international market for proprietary technology, where transfers of technology at present internal to firms are externalised by 'arm's length' contracts between nationals of different countries.

Chapter 1 reviews the basic issues in multinational enterprise – host country relations, and summarises empirical evidence on the subject. The next three chapters develop a theory of the multi-national enterprise. Chapter 2 reviews basic concepts in the theory of resource allocation. Chapter 3 describes how the rationale for the multinational firm originates in industrial economics; various institutions for administering the allocation of resources are compared and the factors which govern the optimum size of firm are determined. Chapter 4 integrates the theory of the firm with the orthodox theory of trade and explains the factors which govern the participation of multinational firms in international trade and investment. The last two chapters are concerned with policy issues. Chapter 5 appraises the costs and benefits of foreign direct investment. Chapter 6 assesses the potential scope for alternatives to foreign direct investment and appraises the relative merits of licensing, subcontracting and other forms of arm's length contractual relationship. Proposals are made for changes in the international patent system.

Acknowledgements

In writing this book I have benefited from discussions with many people. I am particularly grateful to V. N. Balasubramanyam, Peter Buckley, Professor John Creedy, Professor John Dunning, Paul Geroski, Michael Mathew, Bob Pearce, Howard Petith, Alan Rugman and Bernard Wolf. Preliminary versions of the material have been presented to the AUTE Conference at Swansea, the AIB Conference at Bradford, and to seminars at Bradford Management Centre, Nuffield College, Oxford, the University of Southampton and the University of York.

Barbara Wall, Margaret Lewis, Meg Wells, Margaret Fillingham and Joan Horton typed the manuscript with meticulous care.

My wife has read through the manuscript and has done her best to represent the interests of the non-specialist reader.

July 1978   M.C.C.

1 Statement of the issues

1.1 CHANGING ATTITUDES TO THE MULTINATIONAL ENTERPRISE

A multinational enterprise (MNE) is an enterprise which owns and controls assets in more than one country.[1] There is nothing very new about MNEs. They have played a significant role in the world economy since the early seventeenth century, when English and Dutch chartered companies held monopolies of colonial trade, and operated plantations for the export of food and raw materials.[2] As the trading companies declined in the nineteenth century there was a compensating growth of European overseas investment in mining and textiles (and later in oil). The modern style of MNE is a comparatively recent phenomenon, the main impetus for its growth being the opportunities for adapting the advanced technologies of the Second World War to produce consumer goods for world markets. US firms took the lead in the 1950s but European and Japanese firms are now almost on level terms.[3]

Recently there has been increasing concern about the impact of MNEs on host economies.[4] However it can be argued that from the host country's point of view the character of the MNE has changed little since its inception over three hundred years ago.

Firstly, the MNE has always been a monopoly, protected against competitors by 'barriers to entry'. The old-style MNE had a monopoly protected by charter, whereas the new-style MNE has a monopoly upheld by patent rights, branded products or access to specialised managerial skills.

Secondly, because of their monopoly position, MNEs often control key industries or sectors of the host economy. The old-style MNE usually controlled agriculture and mining, whereas the new-style MNE typically controls high-technology manufacturing industries such as chemicals and electronics.

Thirdly, MNEs as a group possess significant control over foreign trade. This is obvious in the case of the chartered trading

1

companies, but still applies today because of the restrictions which many MNEs impose on 'tied inputs' of imported raw materials and intermediate products, and the control they exercise over exports of finished products.

Fourthly, MNEs have largely failed to diffuse know-how to the indigenous populations of less developed countries (LDCs). The old-style MNE drew managers and skilled workers from the colonial expatriate population; the modern MNE is perhaps less dependent on expatriates, but partly because advances in communication enable it to centralise managerial activities at headquarters in the source country.

Finally, foreign investments of MNEs have traditionally been directed into areas where the source country holds military or political influence. This is self-evident in the case of colonial enterprises, but is still discernible today. Its positive aspect is evident in the strength of cross-investment flows within the NATO countries (predominantly the US and Western Europe); its negative aspect appears in the relative decline of foreign direct investment (FDI) in developing countries following decolonisation.

Given the similarities between old- and new-style MNEs, it may be asked why it is only in the postwar period that the relation between MNEs and host countries has become a subject of widespread concern.

One reason is the rapid growth of MNEs, which has turned the leading firms into economic units larger than some host nations. The larger MNEs are also very diverse in their operations; some of them operate in more than one hundred countries. Many MNEs are now internationally owned, which means that the managers who control them are not solely accountable to any one government.

Another factor is the difference between technology-based and resource-based MNEs. In the postwar period MNEs have been increasingly involved in high-technology activities which require skilled labour, in contrast to resource-based activities which make intensive use of unskilled labour. Thus there is a tendency for MNEs' investments to create little additional employment for unskilled workers, who are usually in excess supply in poorer host countries. Instead investment is channelled into richer countries where skilled labour is more abundant. In cases where MNEs have invested in poorer countries their demands for skilled workers have tended to widen income differentials between workers, and thereby exaggerate what is often already a very unequal distribution of income.

Technology-based industries are also more 'footloose' than resource-based industries, and so the bargaining power of host country interests against MNEs has been significantly weakened. It is difficult for any one host government to enforce accountability when the firm can easily liquidate its investments and move elsewhere.

Perhaps the main reason for increasing concern about MNE-host country relations is not the changing character of FDI, but a fundamental change in attitudes towards it. Until fairly recently it was only LDCs that hosted substantial FDI. But the rapid growth of US overseas investments, particularly since the end of the Second World War, has been concentrated in developed countries: Canada, Australia, the United Kingdom and latterly the European Economic Community. This has compelled the developed countries to adopt a different perspective on FDI. At the same time the growth of nationalist sentiment in the developing countries has generated a large critical literature concerned mainly with the political and social consequences of FDI to the host economy. These twin movements have shifted the emphasis of discussions of FDI away from the source country perspective and towards the host country view.

1.2   THE BENEFITS OF FOREIGN DIRECT INVESTMENT

To obtain a balanced view of FDI the problems discussed above have to be offset against the advantages to the host economy.

FDI is distinguished from other forms of foreign investment by the fact that it involves not only foreign ownership but also foreign control. A foreign *direct* investor owns a controlling equity interest in host country assets, whereas a foreign *indirect* investor does not.

Until recently it was believed that the benefits of FDI to the host economy were similar to the benefits of foreign investment in general: they represented the host country's share of the efficiency gains from transferring capital from capital-abundant countries to capital-scarce countries. FDI was perceived simply as a substitute for trade: capital movements equalised international opportunity costs of capital in the same way as did trade according to comparative advantage. It was argued that host country policy toward FDI could be based on an analogy with the optimal tariff argument: the host government should impose an 'optimal tax' on foreign investment income, which would be equivalent to the tariff on the imports for which the investment substituted.[5]

This view of FDI has lost credibility in the postwar era. Only a small proportion of FDI flows between capital-abundant and capital-scarce countries; most of it flows between one capital-abundant country and another – and in both directions at once! Moreover FDI is often associated with offsetting flows of indirect investment, as when a foreign investor takes over an indigenous firm using capital raised in the host country's capital market. Since FDI can take place without any net movement of funds between the two countries concerned, FDI cannot be regarded simply as a component of foreign investment. It follows that the gains from FDI are not merely a special case of the gains from foreign investment in general.

If the role of FDI is not to transfer capital, then what precisely is its role? Students of US investment in Europe were the first to suggest that its role was the transfer of technology. Technology is transferred by establishing a foreign subsidiary which utilises techniques not available to indigenous competitors; as noted above (section 1.1) the technology does not necessarily diffuse beyond the subsidiary.

In the days of the 'technology gap' a fairly narrow definition of technology was applied, but subsequent experience suggests that the definition needs to be widened to include managerial and marketing skills as well as purely technical innovation. The technology transfer view was assimilated into a theory of the 'monopolistic advantages' of the foreign investor; the monopolistic advantages explained why a foreign subsidiary controlled from a distant headquarters could compete with indigenous firms more familiar with the local environment.[6] What the theory failed to explain, however, was why, given the costs of operating at a distance, the monopolistic advantages were not exploited by licensing to indigenous producers. Furthermore the theory had nothing to say about the rationale for the more traditional form of vertically-integrated foreign investment in the food processing, mineral and textile industries.

Both of these problems have been solved by the theory of internalisation, which explains how market imperfections create an incentive for international control of production. The theory is summarised in Chapter 3. According to the theory, the advantage of FDI to the host economy is that it provides institutions which replace external markets and function more efficiently. In particular, FDI provides an internal market mechanism for the transfer of technology to the host economy, and also for the co-ordination of host country activities which form part of an international multi-stage production process. Thus the gain to the host country from FDI is not related principally to the transfer of capital, but to transfers of technology and to investments in multi-stage production *which would not otherwise take place because of external market imperfections.*

1.3 THE SHARE OF FOREIGN DIRECT INVESTMENT GOING TO LESS DEVELOPED COUNTRIES

The following sections of this chapter review empirical evidence on MNE-host country relations. The discussion is oriented toward relations between MNEs and LDCs, since it is on this subject that most recent controversy has centred.

For statistical purposes FDI may be defined as the change in the value of the assets of majority-owned foreign affiliates of domestically registered companies. When interpreting the statistics two important qualifications must be borne in mind. Firstly, book values of assets depend critically on the accounting principles used in valuation, and such conventions often differ considerably between companies. Secondly, the economic value of an asset changes continually in response to changes in replacement cost, interest rates, exchange rates, etc, but changes which occur subsequent to the installation of the asset are not always reflected in its book value. In periods of inflation or currency revaluation in the host country this may create a downward bias in the valuation of older foreign assets.

It is difficult to decide which countries qualify as LDCs.[7] A simple economic criterion is low Gross National Product (GNP) per head. However if the distribution of income is unequal a very large proportion of the population may be poor even though GNP per head is reasonably high. For this reason social, demographic and nutritional indicators are often used to modify or replace the GNP criterion. In geographical terms LDCs may be identified with Latin America, Africa, the Middle East, Asia and the Pacific region, and developed countries with North America and non-communist Europe. The main exceptions are that Australia, New Zealand, Japan, South Africa and some of the Gulf States are developed, while certain Southern European states are LDCs. Approximately three-quarters of the world's population live in LDCs.

By far the largest foreign direct investor in LDCs (as elsewhere) is the United States. It is estimated that just over half the total stock of FDI in LDCs is US-controlled, with the UK, Netherlands, West Germany, Japan, Italy and France (in that order) accounting for over 80% of the remainder.[8] US investment in LDCs is concentrated in Latin America, with the Pacific (Indonesia, Philippines, etc) the next most important area. UK investment is concentrated in Commonwealth countries in Africa and Asia – especially India. Continental European investment in LDCs is directed mainly to former French, Belgian and Dutch colonies in Africa, while Japanese investment is mainly in Southeast Asia.[9]

Despite the widespread existence of labour surpluses in LDCs,

TABLE 1.1. United States direct investment abroad: geographical distribution of the capital stock in 1976 ($, 000m)

Country	Capital stock	Percentage
All countries	137.2	100.0
Developed countries	101.1	73.7
Canada	33.9	24.7
Europe	55.9	40.7
EEC	44.0	32.1
Other Europe	11.9	8.7
Japan	3.8	2.8
Australia and New Zealand	5.9	4.3
South Africa	1.7	1.2
Less developed countries	29.0	21.1
Latin America	23.5	17.1
Africa	2.8	2.0
Middle East	−3.2	−2.3
Asia and Pacific	5.9	4.3

Source: O. G. Whichard and J. N. Freidlin, 'US direct investment abroad in 1975', *Survey of Current Business*, 57, No. 8 (August 1977).
Note: The figure for all countries excludes assets held in international agencies or not allocated.

a relatively small proportion of FDI is directed toward these countries. The latest figures for the US show that in 1976 a mere 21 % of corporate capital abroad was located in LDCs (Table 1.1). Earlier data suggest that a somewhat larger proportion of European investment is directed to LDCs.[10] However the overall picture is incompatible with the view that FDI flows from capital-abundant countries to capital-scarce countries; rather FDI flows *between* capital-abundant countries, with LDCs having a relatively peripheral role.

In fact in the 1960s and early 1970s the proportion of developed countries' FDI directed to LDCs declined. The UK experience is highlighted in Table 1.2, which shows that while corporate capital in LDCs increased by 74%, that in the developed countries as a whole increased by 268%, in the US by 323% and in the EEC by 704%.

However recent experience suggests that this trend may have reversed.[11] Since 1973, United States FDI has increased rapidly in two main fields. Firstly, high oil prices have increased the working capital requirements of the petroleum industry in Latin

TABLE 1.2. United Kingdom direct investment abroad: comparison of the geographical distribution of the capital stock in 1962 and 1974 (current prices)

	1962		1974		% increase 1962–74
	£m	%	£m	%	
All countries	3405	100.0	10118	100.0	197
Developed countries	2163	63.5	7964	78.7	268
Canada	484	14.2	941	9.3	94
US	301	8.4	1273	12.6	323
EEC	273	8.0	2196	21.7	704
EFTA	83	2.4	377	3.7	354
Australia and New Zealand	629	18.5	1931	19.1	207
South Africa	290	8.5	1004	9.9	246
Less developed countries	1241	36.4	2154	21.3	74
India	260	7.6	275	2.7	6
Malaysia	127	3.7	271	2.7	113
Caribbean, Central and South America	277	8.1	464	4.6	68
Africa	414	12.2	737	7.3	78

Source: Trade and Industry (25 February 1977), Table 1, p. 528.

America and the Middle East, and secondly there has been a significant increase in investment in non-manufacturing industries in Latin America. It may therefore be a consequence of the energy crisis and the associated recession in the developed economies that foreign investors are paying more attention to oil- and mineral-rich LDCs.

1.4 THE DISTRIBUTION OF FOREIGN DIRECT INVESTMENT BY INDUSTRY

Three sectors of an economy are usually distinguished, each consisting of a number of industries. The primary sector includes agriculture and the extraction of raw materials and fossil fuels, the secondary sector embraces manufacturing industries, while the tertiary sector includes utilities, transport and distribution, commerce and other services. Typically the primary sector of an LDC is relatively large and the secondary sector relatively small.

TABLE 1.3. Distribution of US foreign direct investment by industry: capital stock in December 1976 ($,000m)

Industry	All countries	Developed countries	Less developed countries	International and unallocated
All industries	137.2	101.1	29.0	7.0
Mining and smelting	7.1	4.7	2.3	0.0
Petroleum	29.7	23.7	2.9	3.9
Manufacturing	61.1	49.7	11.4	0.0
Food	5.1	4.1	1.0	0.0
Chemicals	12.1	9.3	2.8	0.0
Metals	3.8	2.9	0.9	0.0
Machinery	17.0	14.3	2.8	0.0
Transport equipment	9.7	8.5	1.2	0.0
Other	13.3	10.7	2.6	0.0
Transport, communication, utilities	3.2	1.0	0.6	1.7
Trade	13.7	9.9	3.2	0.6
Finance	16.4	8.9	6.0	1.5
Other industries	6.1	3.2	2.7	0.1

Source: O. G. Whichard and J. N. Freidlin, 'US direct investment abroad in 1975', *Survey of Current Business*, 57, No. 8, (August 1977), Table 14.

Published statistics do not permit an exact breakdown of FDI by sectors and industries; in particular disaggregation is usually insufficient to avoid classifying some industries under a large miscellaneous category spanning more than one sector. Subject to this qualification, Table 1.3 suggests that, over all countries, approximately 28% of US FDI is in the primary sector, 47% in the secondary sector, and 25% in the tertiary sector. For LDCs these percentages are respectively 20, 43 and 37. UK FDI presents a similar picture. According to Table 1.4, over all countries approximately 11% is in the primary sector, 61% in the secondary sector and 28% in the tertiary sector, while for LDCs these percentages are respectively 16, 41 and 43.

The relatively low proportion of FDI directed to the manufacturing sector in LDCs is entirely accounted for by the small size of this sector in LDCs. In fact the proportion of overall host country investments accounted for by FDI tends to be greatest

TABLE 1.4. Distribution of UK foreign direct investment by industry: capital stock in December 1974 ($m.)

Industry	All countries	Less developed countries	Commonwealth
Agriculture	462	339	413
Mining and quarrying	662	101	439
Food, drink and tobacco	1552	397	477
Chemical and allied industries	1153	193	445
Metal manufacture	273	25	194
Electrical engineering	667	123	336
Mechanical engineering	487	38	137
Aircraft and shipbuilding	68	n.a.	31
Motor vehicle manufacture	142	n.a.	59
Textiles, clothing and footwear	434	92	149
Paper, printing and publishing	440	43	213
Rubber	150	53	47
Other manufacturing	652	163	282
Construction	123	41	71
Transport and communication	224	144	91
Shipping	133	71	92
Distribution	1687	418	569
Financial services	−28	110	31
Property owning and management	312	63	233
Other activities	524	182	196

Source: Trade and Industry (25 February 1977), Table 3, pp. 532–3.

TABLE 1.5. Foreign ownership in Brazil, 1972

Industry	Percentage of foreign participation
Primary	6.5
Agriculture	7.1
Mineral extraction	6.2
Petroleum	9.6
Secondary	21.6
Non-metallic mineral processing	14.4
Iron and steel	6.8
Other metal processing	16.3
Mechanical engineering	26.1
Electrical and communication equipment	98.1
Vehicles	50.9
Aircraft and shipbuilding	15.8
Wood products	2.7
Cellulose and paper	15.9
Rubber	74.8
Chemicals	46.1
Pharmaceuticals	84.3
Perfumes, soaps, etc	54.7
Plastics	11.9
Textiles	9.0
Clothing, shoes and fabrics	3.5
Food processing	10.5
Beverages	5.3
Tobacco	61.9
Editorial and graphic	3.4
Sundry industrials	0.8
Tertiary	2.3
Electric power	2.4
Investment and development banks	1.2
Commercial banks	2.0
Insurance companies	5.3
Commerce	8.2
Publicity and tourism	1.5
Other services	1.5
TOTAL	9.0

Source: W. L. Ness Jr, 'Brazil: Local equity participation in multinational enterprises', *Law and Policy in International Business*, 1974, 1017–57.

in the manufacturing sector. For example Table 1.5 shows that in Brazil 22% of manufacturing output is controlled by foreign firms but only 7% of primary output and 2% of tertiary output.

There are significant differences among source countries in the distribution of FDI within the manufacturing sector.

US FDI tends to be concentrated in a few industries, most of which may be characterised as 'high technology'. An industry is said to be high technology if R and D expenditure per unit value added is relatively large (as measured by US statistics). In Table 1.3 chemicals, machinery and transport equipment are high-technology industries, and it can be seen that US FDI is higher in these industries than it is in the low-technology industries of food and metals.

In economies where most FDI is sourced by the US this pattern shows up in the figures for aggregate foreign participation in various industries. In Brazil for example (Table 1.5) foreign participation is highest in electrical and communication equipment, pharmaceutical products, rubber, perfumes, vehicles and 'other chemicals' – all high-technology industries – and lowest in wood products, editorial and graphics, clothing, beverages and textiles – all low-technology industries. The only exceptions are that foreign participation is high in tobacco and low in petroleum.

In contrast UK manufacturing investment typically represents backward integration by firms engaged in manufacturing consumer products. Although high-technology industries such as chemicals and electrical engineering figure prominently in UK FDI, the most important industries are food and distribution (see Table 1.4).

Differences between source countries in the industrial distribution of FDI are highlighted in Table 1.6, which refers to the Brazilian economy in 1973. It shows that while US investment predominates in machinery and chemicals, UK investment predominates in agriculture and food processing, Japanese investment in textiles, and Canadian investment in banking and insurance. West German investment is concentrated in machinery while Swiss investment is in food and chemicals.

We may tentatively conclude that not only is FDI particularly prominent in certain manufacturing industries, but there is a real sense in which individual industries in LDCs are strongly dependent on investment controlled from a single source country.[12]

1.5 THE SIGNIFICANCE OF FOREIGN DIRECT INVESTMENT IN THE INTERNATIONAL CAPITAL MARKET

Within the international capital market FDI is just one component of total investment, other major components being private long-

TABLE 1.6. Industrial distribution of the stock of foreign direct investment by source country in Brazil, December 1973 ($ million 6.2 cruzeiros per dollar)

Source country	Agriculture and food processing	Mineral and mineral processing	INDUSTRY Machinery and electrical	Chemical and pharma-ceutical	Textiles	Banking and insurance	Commerce and services	TOTAL $ Millions	%
United States	174.1	436.0	987.7	547.1	27.1	114.3	60.4	2346.8	45
West Germany	23.3	92.6	395.9	141.6	3.9	12.9	18.8	689.1	13
United Kingdom	234.4	6.3	26.7	24.1	18.7	40.2	12.3	362.8	7
Japan	4.8	67.6	103.2	6.8	40.4	83.7	53.2	359.8	7
Canada	5.2	32.9	30.3	–	–	247.9	1.0	317.3	6
Switzerland	70.9	16.3	39.7	77.1	4.1	17.2	11.5	237.0	5
Other	n.a.	n.a.	n.a.	n.a.	n.a.	n.a.	n.a.	n.a.	17
Total recorded*	512.9	651.8	1583.6	796.7	94.3	516.3	157.2	4312.2	83
Percentage distribution	11.9	15.2	36.7	18.5	2.2	12.0	3.6	100.0	–
Estimated total	n.a.	n.a.	n.a.	n.a.	n.a.	n.a.	n.a.	5200.0	100

n.a. = not available.
*Thought to represent approximately 80% of the total, which is estimated at $5.2 billion.
Source: R. D. Robinson, *National Control of Foreign Business Entry: A Survey of Fifteen Countries*, New York, 1976, Table 7.7.

TABLE 1.7. Foreign assets owned by US citizens, December 1975 ($ million)

Type of asset	Amount	Percentage of total
Total assets abroad	304,110	100.0
Official reserve assets	16,226	5.3
Other US government assets	41,808	13.7
Private assets	246,076	80.9
Direct investments	133,168	43.8
Foreign securities	35,159	11.6
Debenture	25,577	8.4
Minority equity	9582	3.2
Non-bank claims	18,298	6.0
Bank claims	59,451	19.5

Source: R. B. Scholl, 'The international investment position of the US: Developments in 1975', *Survey of Current Business*, 56, No. 8 (August 1976), Table 3.

term investments in debentures and equities – so-called 'portfolio investments' – private short-term investments, government investments, and holdings of official reserve assets. Table 1.7 shows the significance of FDI in total US assets abroad at the end of 1975. FDI is approximately 54% of all US private foreign investment, compared with 10% accounted for by debentures and a mere 4% by minority equity participation in overseas enterprises. Private assets account for 81% of all US assets abroad, making FDI 44% of the total US credit position with the rest of the world.

Relations between developed and less developed countries in the international capital market are summarised in Table 1.8, which gives details of the flows of funds in 1976. Developed countries are identified as members of the Development Assistance Committee (DAC); flows are measured net of LDC investment in DAC countries. [13] Private flows of investment from DAC members account for 55% of total net investment; direct investment is in turn 34% of the private flow, the other main components being bilateral portfolio investment (27%) and private export credits (24%). Overall, direct investment is 19% of total net investment in LDCs. As such it is equivalent to half the official development assistance, and to over twice the other official flows.

The significance of direct investment varies marginally between source countries. As might be expected it is high in countries with

TABLE 1.8. Net flows of financial resources from member countries of the Development Assistance Committee (DAC) to less developed countries, 1976

Category of investment	DAC total	UK	US	West Germany
Total net investment	40,505	2176	12,344	5314
Official development assistance (ODA)	13,656	835	4334	1384
Bilateral ODA	9495	580	2838	1044
Grants and similar contributions	6529	565	1684	512
Development lending and capital	2966	15	1154	532
Contributions to multilateral institutions	4161	254	1496	340
Grants	1933	109	394	282
Capital subscription payments	2166	143	1102	35
Concessional lending	61	1	0	23
Other official flows (OOF)	3305	31	822	43
Bilateral OOF	3186	31	822	15
Official export credits	1823	0	814	−29
Debt reorganisation	80	0	13	37
Equities, etc	1283	31	−5	0
Contributions to multilateral institutions	119	0	0	27
IBRD	18	0	0	21
Other	101	0	0	6
Private flows	22,186	1263	6399	3682
Private investment and lending	16,762	845	6575	2834
Direct investment	7593	722	3119	765
New Investment	n.a.	n.a.	1850	487
Reinvested earnings	n.a.	n.a.	1269	278
Bilateral portfolio investment etc	6072	123	2160	1138
Multilateral portfolio investment	3097	0	1296	930
Private export credits	5424	418	−176	848
Grants by voluntary agencies	1358	47	789	205

Note: All figures $ million.
Source: OECD, *Development Co-operation 1977*, Paris, 1977, Table A10, p. 174.

colonial traditions such as the UK (33%), and below average for other countries, such as West Germany (14%).

The net inflow of capital to LDCs benefits the host country in the long term through an increase in productive potential, and also in the short term by increasing demand for the host currency, and thereby reducing the foreign-exchange cost of imports. However a net inflow of capital also creates long-term costs due to the repatriation of interest and dividends; repatriation can also cause short-term problems if speculative factors lead to the raising of dividend pay-out ratios or non-renewal of debenture lending. It is therefore of particular interest to determine whether the flow of FDI to LDCs is always sufficient to finance flows of dividends and other remittances.

Table 1.9 illustrates the impact of FDI on the US balance of payments, using data for 1976. The net contribution of FDI to the US balance of payments in 1976 is measured by the difference between the remittance of foreign earnings (on income account) and the net financing of new FDI (on capital account). In fact this understates the contribution to the extent that remittance of royalties and management fees are excluded (for details of these see the next section). The figures show this net contribution to be positive: $1.8 billion being paid to the US by developed countries and $4.1 billion by the LDCs. Thus in 1976 LDCs had to finance a deficit of $4.1 billion either by other forms of borrowing or by running a trade surplus with the US or its creditors. There is thus a real problem for LDCs in that new US financing of FDI – through either capital flows or retained profits – does not match the foreign earnings of US subsidiaries. This phenomenon is not particularly new; it has been apparent for the past ten years or so.[14]

There are two further points worth noting from Table 1.9. The first is that a high proportion of total earnings in LDCs are remitted: 83%, as against 46% for earnings originating in developed countries. This may present difficulties in the short run, since fluctuations in the profits of foreign subsidiaries may induce significant movements in the host country balance of payments. However an enforced change in remittance policy is unlikely to yield a long-term benefit, since in the aggregate it will induce a compensating change in the volume of new external financing of FDI.

The second point is that, in view of the book values of investment quoted in Table 1.1, the earnings figures suggest a much

TABLE 1.9. Balance of payments effects of the earnings of US foreign direct investment by category of host nation, 1976 ($,000 million)

| Variable | All countries | Category of host country | | |
		Developed countries	Less developed countries	International and unallocated
1. Foreign earnings	18.8	11.4	7.0	0.5
2. Remitted earnings	11.1	5.2	5.8	0.1
3. Reinvested earnings	7.7	6.2	1.2	0.3
4. Net foreign investment	12.3	9.6	2.9	−0.1
5. Net capital movement	4.6	3.4	1.7	−0.4
Net contribution to US balance of payments = 1−4 = 2−5	6.5	1.8	4.1	0.6

Source: O. G. Whichard and J. N. Freidlin, 'US direct investment abroad in 1976, *Survey of Current Business*, 57, No. 8 (August 1977), Tables 14–22.

TABLE 1.10. US and UK average returns on book value of foreign direct investment by area, 1965–8 (percentages)

Host country	US All sectors	US Excluding petroleum	UK Excluding petroleum
Developed countries	7.9	9.6	9.3
US	–	–	8.6
Canada	8.0	8.6	11.3
Europe (non-communist)	7.1	10.0	7.9
Japan	14.2	20.2	n.a.
Australia, New Zealand and South Africa	9.7	12.0	9.5
Less developed countries	17.5	11.0	9.8
Western hemisphere	12.1	11.1	8.7
Asia	34.7	11.7	} 10.4
Africa	22.3	7.7	
Europe			
Unallocated	8.5	11.6	

Source: United Nations: *Multinational Corporations in World Development*, New York, 1973, Table 37.

higher rate of return on investment in LDCs than in developed countries.

This is corroborated by Table 1.10. Given the high rate of return in LDCs we should expect a relatively high rate of investment in LDCs, which we have seen previously is not the case. One probable explanation is that foreign investors perceive high risks in investments in LDCs so that the risk premium on investment offsets the higher rate of return. If this conjecture is correct it suggests that so long as these perceptions remain LDCs will continue to experience difficulty in financing remittances with new externally funded direct investments.

1.6 PAYMENTS FOR TECHNOLOGY

It is widely recognised that one of the main roles of multinational firms is as a vehicle for technology transfer. This ties in with the observation in section 1.4 that foreign direct investments predominate in the high technology areas of manufacturing industry. The sale of proprietary technologies generates a stream of royalties

TABLE 1.11. US receipts of fees and royalties from foreign direct investment, 1975–6 ($ million)

Country	Royalties and licence fees	Other income	Total
All countries	1886	1657	3543
Developed countries	1707	1063	2770
Canada	198	368	566
EEC	1090	443	1532
Other European	150	83	233
Japan	171	52	223
Australia, New Zealand and South Africa	99	118	216
Less developed countries	173	549	722
Latin America	115	262	376
Africa	19	79	97
Middle East	4	125	130
Asia and Pacific	35	83	118
International and unallocated	6	45	51

Source: O. G. Whichard and J. N. Freidlin, 'US direct investment abroad in 1976,' *Survey of Current Business*, 57, No. 8 (August 1977), Table 11.
Note: Royalties and fees consist of payments for the sale or use of intangible property such as patents, processes, trademarks and copyrights; other income consists of management fees, service charges, film and television tape rentals, and rentals for tangible property.

and licence fees. By far the largest recipient of royalties and fees is the US. Other major recipients are West Germany, France, UK and Japan.[15]

Table 1.11 gives a breakdown of US receipts from proprietary information by country of origin. Payments of royalties and licence fees are contrasted with payments for other property rights, such as management fees and miscellaneous rentals. It can be seen that although on a global scale royalty payments are extremely high (and constitute a major credit in the US balance of payments), the proportion exacted from LDCs is less than 10%, although LDC payments for other property rights are much higher and constitute a third of total US income from this source.

Students of development often focus on the balance of payment costs of royalty payments by LDCs, but the evidence suggests that in relation to remitted foreign earnings, royalty payments are of little significance. In fact it is likely that the statistics overstate

TABLE 1.12. Analysis of payments by LDCs for the transfer of technology

| Country | Date | Payment ($m. equivalent, current prices) | | | Payments as % of | |
		Patents, trademarks, etc	Management services etc	Total	GDP	Exports
Argentina	1970	70.5	45.3	115.8	0.49	6.5
Brazil	1970	n.a.	n.a.	104.0	0.29	3.8
Chile	1969	8.2	n.a.	(8.2)	0.13	0.8
Colombia	1966	n.a.	n.a.	26.7	0.49	5.3
Mexico	1968	n.a.	n.a.	200.0	0.74	15.9
Peru	1971	9.9	1.1	11.0	0.19	1.2
Venezuela	1966	14.8	n.a.	(14.8)	0.17	0.5
Nigeria	1965	19.0	14.8	33.8	0.72	4.5
India	1969	6.4	43.2	49.6	0.10	2.7
Indonesia	1968	25.0	n.a.	(25.0)	0.23	3.6
Iran	1970	1.7	1.6	3.3	0.03	0.1
Israel	1961–5	1.6	2.3	3.9	0.15	1.2
Republic of Korea	1970	2.1	n.a.	(2.1)	0.03	0.3
Pakistan	1965–70	2.1	(100.0)	(102.1)	0.70	15.7
Sri Lanka	1970	0.1	9.2	9.3	0.42	2.7
Greece	1966	n.a.	n.a.	2.6	0.04	0.6
Spain	1970	81.6	52.2	133.8	0.41	5.6
Turkey	1968	n.a.	n.a.	49.1	0.39	9.9
Yugoslavia	1970	5.4	n.a.	(5.4)	0.04	0.3
Total		n.a.	n.a.	900.5	0.32	3.8

Source: UNCTAD, *Major Issues arising from the Transfer of Technology to Developing Countries*, New York: United Nations TD/B/AC.11/10/Rev. 2, Table 10.
Note: Figures in brackets are estimated quantities.

true royalty payments because dividends are often disguised as royalties to reduce taxable income.[16] In view of this it cannot be said that the real cost of importing technology into LDCs is prohibitively high. Table 1.12 indicates that even when payments of management fees and miscellaneous rentals are included, there is no instance within a sample of eighteen LDCs where payments exceed 0.75% of the host country GNP. Indeed it will be one of the main arguments of this book that the major barrier to the transfer of technology to LDCs is not the cost to the host country, but the unwillingness of source-country firms to license or invest because of the difficulty of appropriating a reasonable share of the wealth created by the technology.

1.7 RESTRICTIVE BUSINESS PRACTICES IN THE TRANSFER OF TECHNOLOGY

Contracts relating to the transfer of technology usually contain clauses limiting the freedom of the licensee (whether indigenous firm or foreign subsidiary) to exploit the technology. Three of the most common types of restriction are quotas or prohibitions on exports, obligations to purchase key inputs from the licensor and obligations to offer technical improvements back to the licensor.

It is easy to see why such restrictions are to the advantage of the licensor. Restrictions on exports from the host economy permit the licensor to segment the world market and charge according to 'what the market will bear' in each segment, thereby achieving the maximum possible return from his monopoly of the technology. Obligations to purchase key inputs enable the licensor to monitor the activities of the licensee; in particular the licensee's demand for the key input provides an independent check on the production figures quoted by the licensee when determining his royalty payment. The obligation to offer back technical improvements protects the licensor against obsolescence arising from marginal technical improvements implemented by the licensee.

Perhaps the most pervasive restrictions relate to exports. Table 1.13 shows that in many countries (six out of ten in the table) more than half of all contracts impose export restrictions on the licensor; in Peru, Mexico and Chile more than 90% of all contracts do so. Restrictive clauses are analysed in depth in Table 1.14, which relates to contracts registered with foreign investment

TABLE 1.13. Percentages of contracts containing restrictive export clauses c. 1970

Country	Percentage
Peru	99
Mexico	97
Chile	93
Bolivia	83
Colombia	79
Ecuador	75
India	43
Philippines	32
Argentina	28
Israel	6

Source: UNCTAD, *Major Issues arising from the Transfer of Technology to Developing Countries*, New York: United Nations, TD/B/AC. 11/10/Rev. 2, Table 7.

review bodies (or similar agencies) in India, the Philippines and Mexico. In India most export restrictions relate to specific foreign markets whereas in the Philippines and Mexico a global ban on exports is the most common. Restrictions on tied purchases and improvements to the licensor are much more common in the Philippines than in the other two countries. In Mexico restrictions on the use of trademarks in exports and restrictions on the production pattern are common. It is clear that there are substantial differences in the types of restriction faced by different countries; these almost certainly reflect differences in the type of product manufactured under licence in each country.

It appears to be a widely held view that the insertion of restrictive clauses in contracts for technology transfer is the outcome of a bargaining process in which a skilled negotiator (the proprietor) takes advantage of the licensee. It is argued that the bargaining is bound to favour the proprietor since he knows more about the technology than does the prospective licensee.[17] The way to correct this inequality of bargaining power is said to be for potential host countries – in particular the LDCs – to collude in their bargaining with the proprietor and collectively to insist that they will not accept restrictions of this kind.

TABLE 1.14. Analysis of restrictive clauses in three LDCs

	Country		
Type of restrictive clause	India (1969)	Philippines (1970)	Mexico (1969)
Export restrictions	161	82	106
Global ban on exports	3	49	53
Exports prohibited to specific countries	60	4	3
Exports permitted to specified countries only	60	1	1
Prior approval for exports	15	17	13
Export quotas	–	–	5
Price control on exports	–	–	4
Exports permitted to or through specified firms only	16	6	12
Restrictions on use of trademarks in exports	5	5	15
Other restrictions			
Tied purchases	16	67	1
Restrictions on production pattern	–	5	19
Payment of minimum royalty	4	13	–
Restriction on sales procedures	1	–	–
Improvements to licensor	–	14	–
Restrictions on termination	–	3	–
External adjudication of legal disputes	–	21	–
Total number of restrictive agreements	171	126	109

Source: UNCTAD, *Restrictive Business Practices: Interim Report*, New York: United Nations TD/B/C.2/104/Rev. 1, Tables 2–4.
Note: The total number of export restrictions and other restrictions can exceed the total number of agreements with restrictions because a given agreement can contain an export restriction as well as other types of restriction. A given agreement can also contain one or more types of export restriction.

It is certainly true that in the past the lack of bargaining skills in LDCs has led them to accept very unfavourable terms from MNEs.[18] However it can be argued that many of the restrictive clauses in technology contracts are a legitimate defence of the proprietor's interests, so much so that if host countries outlaw such practices proprietors may prefer to abstain from FDI or licensing rather than meet the host country's terms. In fact we shall argue that both export restrictions and the buy-back of

TABLE 1.15. Cross-classification of types of royalty agreement by industry, Philippines, 1970

	Ad valorem royalty				Lump sum or quantity-related royalty	n.a.	TOTAL
	Nominal	1–4.9%	5–10%	More than 10%			
Plantation, mining and petroleum	–	–	–	–	–	1	1
Manufacturing							
Foods	4	7	2	1	3	14	31
Beverages	2	1	7	–	–	9	19
Textiles and wearing apparel	–	–	1	–	2	2	5
Electrical supplies, electrical appliances and accessories	4	1	2	–	–	13	20
Chemicals, paints and paint materials	5	7	8	1	2	1	24
Pharmaceuticals	17	2	30	–	1	8	58
Metals and metal products, and construction equipment and materials	7	3	6	–	5	6	27
Petroleum products	3	–	1	–	1	4	9
Cosmetics, toiletries, soaps and detergents	4	1	2	–	–	12	19
Motors, engines, machinery, distribution transformers	–	4	–	–	–	3	7
Tobacco products	–	–	–	–	3	11	14
Office supplies and equipment	1	–	6	–	–	6	13
Cars, car parts and rubber products	2	–	1	–	4	–	7
Total	49	26	66	2	21	90	254

Source: UNCTAD, *Restrictions on Exports in Foreign Collaboration Agreements in the Republic of the Philippines*, New York: United Nations, TD/B/388, Table 12.

improvements are essential to any efficient market in proprietary information, and that only restrictions on tied inputs can be condemned on efficiency grounds. It is quite possible for host countries to accept these restrictions and still benefit substantially from FDI; they will certainly benefit more than if the supply of technologies dries up because of a refusal to meet the minimal requirements of proprietors.

Contracts for technology transfer are noteworthy not only for the restrictions they impose on the licensee's behaviour but also for the fact that they normally specify royalty payments which are related to output. For example Table 1.15 shows that in the Philippines most royalty payments are on an *ad valorem* basis. Although some royalties are purely nominal the typical rate is between 5% and 10% of the value of the product.

Now technical knowledge is not a resource which is 'used up' in production in the same way as material inputs. It would therefore appear that an *ad valorem* royalty will induce an artificial restriction on the licensee's output; certainly he will produce less than he would were the royalty a lump sum payment independent of output. *Prima facie* this is evidence of a monopolistic restriction of output imposed indirectly by the licensor. As such it may be considered to be a restrictive business practice.

In fact we shall argue that such a restriction is an essential instrument by which the licensor protects the value of his proprietary information when licensing simultaneously to competing licensees. In these circumstances the practice is compatible with efficiency. However there are certainly other instances where the practice is indefensible.

1.8 HOST COUNTRY POLICIES

In the late 1960s it was widely believed that national sovereignty was threatened by the growth of MNEs. To some it seemed that by becoming international, big business had freed itself from social and political accountability. If host country policies did not suit business interests, firms would uproot themselves and transfer investments elsewhere; the economic and political consequences of this might be so severe that the mere threat could be sufficient to modify host government attitudes. To others the growth of MNEs reinforced the view that the nation state was no longer

TABLE 1.16. Host country perception of restrictive business practices by MNEs

Type of restriction	*Turkey*	*Peru*	*Singapore*	*Mexico*	*Nigeria*	*Malta*	*Ecuador*	*Cyprus*	*Pakistan*	*Greece*	*Sri Lanka*	*Chile*	*Argentina*	*Iran*	*Rep. of Korea*	*Yes*	*No*	*No Reply*
Tied purchases of imported inputs, equipment and spare parts	√	√		√	√	√	√	√	√	√	√	√	√		×	12	1	2
Restriction of exports (total prohibition, partial limitation, geographical constraint)	√	√	×	√	√	√	√	√	√	√	√	√	√	√		13	1	1
Requirement of guarantees against changes in taxes, tariffs and exchange rates affecting profits, royalties and remittances	√	×		√	×		√	×						×		3	4	8
Limitation of competing supplies by: (a) restriction of competing imports	×	√	×	√	√	×	√	×	√					×	×	5	6	4
(b) preventing competition for local resources	×	√	×	√			×	√						×	×	3	5	7
(c) obtaining local patents to eliminate competitors	×			√	√	√		×						×		3	3	9
Constraints limiting the dynamic effects of the transfer: (a) excessive use of expatriate personnel	√	√	×	√	√	√								√		6	1	8
(b) discouragement of the development of local technical and research and development capabilities	√	×		√	√	√	√					√		√		7	1	7

Source: UNCTAD, *Major Issues arising from the Transfer of Technology to Developing Countries*, New York: United Nations, TD/B/AC.11/10/Rev. 2, Table 4.

viable as an economic unit; much larger federations of states based on free trade areas were the appropriate units over which to exercise political sovereignty.

In the latter half of the 1970s the picture is very different. The relative growth of MNEs has slowed down for a variety of reasons. Many firms are by now much nearer to what they regard as an optimal degree of international diversification, and are no longer investing in new markets. Also the pace of technological advance – which is a key factor in the growth of MNEs – has slowed down because of reductions in government financing of R and D in developed countries. But another factor has been the rise of nationalist attitudes, particularly in LDCs, which have generated an increasingly hostile attitude to MNEs.

Host governments are particularly sensitive to the restrictive business practices adopted by MNEs. Table 1.16 shows that in a sample of fifteen LDCs, thirteen perceived export restrictions to be a major factor; twelve mentioned tied purchases of inputs, seven the discouragement of local R and D efforts, six the excessive use of expatriate personnel and five the restriction of competing imports.

Many host governments have been active in developing statutes and guidelines governing foreign business entry. A recent survey of fifteen host countries reported that the exercise of national sovereignty over FDI was stronger than ever before; a summary of the findings is presented in Table 1.17. The most common host country requirement is that a certain proportion of equity owner-ship of the foreign subsidiary should be 'spun off' to indigenous investors within a fixed period of time. Some countries impose barriers to foreign entry into certain sectors; for example in Thailand many professions and similar activities are restricted to Thais, and some undertakings have maximum permissible rates of growth while they remain majority foreign-owned. Restrictions on royalty payments are also enforced, most notably in the Andean Common Market where internal royalty payments to a parent firm are prohibited and dividend remittances are restricted to 14% of capital. At the same time host governments offer a number of incentives to foreign investors. The most common are incentives for training native personnel; some countries give subsidies for entry into particular industries while others are willing to accept arbitration by the International Centre for Investment Disputes.

TABLE 1.17. Host country regulation of entry: an analysis of restrictions and incentives in selected LDCs

Country	No foreign direct investment	Spin-off equity	Barriers to entry into certain sectors	Restrictions on royalties and fees	Allows external arbitration	Selective subsidies and incentives	Rewards training
Indonesia		✓			✓		✓
Malaysia		✓			✓		✓
Thailand			✓				✓
Burma	✓						
Philippines						✓	✓
Mexico		✓					
Brazil				✓		✓	
Andean Common Market		✓			✓		

Source: R. D. Robinson, *National Control of Foreign Business Entry: A Survey of Fifteen Countries*, New York, 1976.

1.9 EQUITY AND EFFICIENCY

Although host countries perceive many problems in their relations with MNEs this does not imply that an international economic order based on the transfer of technology by MNEs should be rejected. It must first be demonstrated that a preferable alternative regime exists. The alternative must be feasible: it must not be based on an ideal view of how the world economy works, but must take full account of economic, social and political constraints. A practical alternative must therefore reckon with the conflicts generated by the self-interested pursuit of different individual and national objectives.

The alternatives considered in this book are essentially two-fold: the 'market alternative' which involves substituting for FDI arm's length contractual arrangements such as licensing and sub-contracting, and supranational regulation, which involves the enforcement of an international code of conduct for MNEs.

It is useful to have explicit criteria by which the alternatives can be appraised. The criteria traditionally used by economists are efficiency and equity. Efficiency means that no one is unnecessarily poor; in other words they cannot be made better off without damaging someone else's interests. An efficient international economic order is one in which no resources are wasted – for example by misallocation – so that a poor nation can only be made better off by redistributing wealth from richer nations.

Equity implies that the distribution of income satisfies notions of natural justice. Since concepts of natural justice differ between individuals the notion of an equitable distribution of income is essentially subjective. Much of the debate on the international economic order has been concerned with equity, both between nations, and between different groups within host nations.

The analysis in this book is concerned mainly with efficiency. This is not because equity is unimportant, but because both equity and efficiency are sufficiently important to warrant separate treatment, and it is our belief that previous discussion has paid too little regard to considerations of efficiency.

Theory

2 The concept of efficiency and its application to proprietary information

2.1 INTRODUCTION

This chapter begins by summarising economists' insights into the nature of efficient resource allocation. Section 2.2 introduces the concept of Pareto-efficiency and describes the role of prices in the coordination of economic activities. Section 2.3 considers the use of discriminatory pricing to achieve efficient allocation under increasing returns to scale.

The main part of the chapter applies this analysis to the market for information. Section 2.4 considers the diffusability – or 'public good' nature – of information and argues that discriminatory pricing is normally necessary for its efficient development and use. Section 2.5 introduces the concept of a patent. Section 2.6 considers pricing strategy in a market for a good embodying information in its design or production technology. Section 2.7 considers the problems of licensing information simultaneously to several producers of such goods; it is argued that in certain cases efficiency requires the use of an *ad valorem* royalty system. Section 2.8 considers the problem of preventing wasteful replication of R and D activities and argues that efficiency normally calls for a property right in planned programmes of research as well as in the results of completed research.

Readers familiar with economic literature may wish to skip the early sections of this chapter, or perhaps proceed directly to Chapter 3, and refer back to the later sections where necessary.

2.2 EFFICIENCY AND PRICES[1]

If society consisted of a collection of individuals with truly identical preferences there would be complete consensus on all decisions. But where preferences differ conflicts are likely to emerge because an action which furthers one individual's objectives hinders another's. Members of society will agree only that a strategy which benefits someone without making anyone else worse off is preferable to the *status quo*. A strategy to which no preferable alternative exists is said to be Pareto-efficient. In most cases there exists a whole set of Pareto-efficient strategies, each strategy providing a different distribution of benefits between individuals. The individuals will be unable to agree on which is the best of the efficient strategies; thus any ranking of efficient strategies represents a purely personal value judgement.

The achievement of efficiency depends on the proper co-ordination of resource use. Efficient coordination does not necessarily require a centralised plan; the process of coordination can be decentralised through the use of prices.

Let every input and output of a productive activity be identified as a distinct commodity and let each commodity be traded in a market. In each market all items are exchanged at a uniform price, and each transactor regards the price as a datum which is beyond his own influence (price is 'parametric'). Any individual can transact in any market. Given that each individual optimises with respect to his preferences, he can calculate the net amount he is willing to offer on each market as a function only of the prevailing prices. As a consumer he demands goods and as a factor owner he supplies factor services. Aggregating across transactors in any given market determines total planned demand and total planned supply as functions of the prices. A set of prices which equates demand to supply in every market is said to be an equilibrium set.

It can be shown that under certain conditions an equilibrium set of prices exists, and at any equilibrium the amounts actually transacted represent an efficient allocation of resources. The significance of this result is that much of the responsibility for coordinating individuals' actions can be delegated to individuals themselves. To achieve efficiency it is sufficient for each transactor to reveal to others only the net amounts of each commodity he is willing to supply at the equilibrium prices; it is unnecessary for him to reveal to others the information by which he determines the net amounts he wishes to supply. The only activity which needs to be centralised is the fixing of equilibrium prices, and even this can sometimes be left to negotiations between the transactors (see section 3.2).

The efficiency of equilibrium prices no longer applies when production takes place under increasing returns to scale. An activity exhibits increasing returns to scale when an equiproportional increase in all inputs leads to a larger proportional increase in all outputs. In practice increasing returns to scale is a fairly common phenomenon, and in particular it applies to the exploitation of technology (see section 2.4). Allocation of resources under increasing returns to scale is most easily studied using the partial equilibrium analysis described in the following section.

2.3 INCREASING RETURNS TO SCALE AND PRICE DISCRIMINATION[2]

Partial equilibrium analysis studies the nature of equilibrium in one market when prices in all other markets remain fixed at their equilibrium values. It is usually restricted to markets in which

(i) the commodity has no close substitutes or complements, either in demand or supply, so that a change in its price will not influence significantly prices in other markets, and

(ii) for each individual the net value of his transactions in the market is a small proportion of his total income, so that the income effects of a price change are negligible.

Partial equilibrium analysis provides simple criteria for the efficient quantity traded in a given market. Suppose that initially the quantity traded is restricted to zero, and then gradually increased in a succession of small increments. Marginal benefit is defined as the maximum value the keenest demander is willing to sacrifice in order to acquire a further increment and marginal cost is the minimum value the most able supplier is willing to accept as compensation for it. The excess of marginal benefit over marginal cost measures the surplus created by the incremental transaction. Under the assumed conditions the surpluses generated by different increments are additive; their sum is known as the market surplus, and is a measure of the social welfare generated by transactions in the market.

Both marginal benefit and marginal cost normally vary with the quantity traded. A necessary condition for the maximisation of market surplus is that the quantity traded is such that marginal benefit is equal to marginal cost.

In graphical terms the maximisation of market surplus implies

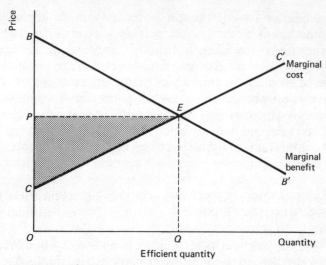

FIGURE 2.1. Market equilibrium with non-increasing returns to scale

that the quantity is chosen to maximise the area lying between the marginal benefit and marginal cost schedules. When consumers have diminishing marginal utility the marginal benefit decreases with respect to quantity. Marginal cost normally increases with respect to quantity, except under increasing returns to scale, when

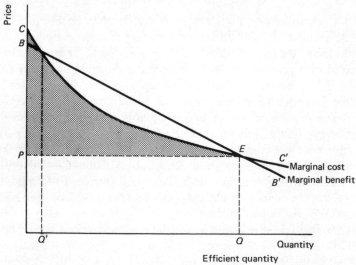

FIGURE 2.2. Market equilibrium with increasing returns to scale

it decreases (cf. Figures 2.1 and 2.2). If marginal cost everywhere exceeds marginal benefit the efficient quantity is zero. If marginal cost is increasing the efficient quantity is determined by the (unique) intersection of the marginal benefit and marginal cost schedules. Under increasing returns the efficient quantity (if positive) corresponds to an intersection, but an arbitrary intersection does not necessarily correspond to an efficient quantity (e.g. in Figure 2.2 the output Q is efficient but Q^1 is not).

When consumers have diminishing marginal utility the marginal benefit schedule coincides with the demand schedule generated by a varying uniform parametric market price. The pricing strategy compatible with efficiency is to set the price so that demand is equal to the efficient quantity. When marginal cost is increasing this price allows suppliers to earn a surplus, measured by the shaded area CEP in Figure 2.1. The surplus arises because total cost (as measured by the area $OCEQ$) is less than the value of transactions in the market (as measured by the area of the rectangle $OPEQ$). But under increasing returns to scale the price which maximises market surplus causes suppliers to make a loss (equal to the shaded area CEP in Figure 2.2). Thus if the supply is voluntary then nothing will be forthcoming, and since the quantity traded cannot exceed the amount supplied, transactions will be zero and the outcome inefficient. This illustrates the general problem posed by increasing returns: the uniform price compatible with an efficient level of demand is incompatible with breaking-even in supply.

One solution to this problem is to abandon uniform prices and to charge a different price for each unit traded; this is known as discriminatory pricing. For discriminatory prices to be efficient they must ensure that the price charged for the marginal unit is equal to its marginal cost of supply and the prices of intramarginal units are such that the profit from supply is positive if and only if the market surplus is positive. These conditions are always satisfied if the pricing scheme is based on the marginal benefit schedule, in which case all of the market surplus is appropriated by the suppliers. This pricing system is not necessary for efficiency – other systems which give less profit to the supplier are also acceptable. In certain cases discriminatory prices can be based on the supply schedule, in which case all the market surplus is appropriated by the demanders. In principle it is possible to secure any distribution of the market surplus by devising the appropriate pricing strategy. In practice it may be simplest to allow suppliers to discriminate on the basis of the marginal benefit curve, and to redistribute some of their profits to demanders through the tax system.

Partial equilibrium analysis therefore suggests that efficient decentralisation of the allocation of resources to increasing-returns activities may be achieved through discriminatory pricing. Price discrimination reconciles low prices on marginal units to encourage demand with high prices on the intramarginal units to permit profitable supply of resource inputs. On these grounds it is unambiguously superior to uniform prices.

2.4 EFFICIENT DEVELOPMENT AND USE OF INFORMATION

In the theoretical sections of this book we prefer to use the concept of information rather than technology. This allows us to bring marketing and managerial skills within the scope of our discussion. It is also appropriate because the economic characteristics of technical information are common to most other types of information as well.

The ultimate use of information – like any other commodity – is to satisfy consumer wants. Wants are satisfied directly when the information is of intrinsic interest to the consumer, and indirectly when the information is embodied in some other form, e.g. a new or improved commodity. The ultimate source of information – like any other commodity – is the utilisation of factors of production, particularly human capital.

It is obvious that when contemplating the acquisition of information the researcher is in a state of uncertainty about the subject of the information. However it will be assumed throughout the analysis that he can foresee the costs of acquiring the information and the economic consequences of utilising it.

To determine in principle whether it is efficient to invest in acquiring a given item of information it is necessary to formulate the constraints on the economy prior to the information becoming available and to contrast these with the constraints on the system after the information has become available. Typically the impact of the information is to relax some constraints and tighten others. For example, development of a new technology raises productivity in the innovating industry, but uses up resources in the research sector.

The characteristics of efficient development and use of information depend crucially on one fundamental property of information, namely its diffusability. Information is diffusable because it can always be made available to another individual without any diminution of existing users' access to it; i.e. in entering one person's comprehension it is not eliminated from someone else's comprehension.[3] As a consequence the development and use of information exhibits increasing returns to scale. The marginal cost of supplying the first user is very high, since it includes all the research costs, but the marginal cost of supplying subsequent users includes only the cost of communication, and in most instances this is relatively small. Partial equilibrium theory (section 2.3) tells us that under increasing returns to scale efficiency can be achieved using discriminatory prices. For example if each final user of the information is charged a price equal to the maximum he is willing to pay, the profit-maximising strategy is to develop the information only if the market surplus is positive and to supply it to all users for whom the marginal benefit exceeds the marginal cost. Thus with discriminatory pricing, profit maximisation leads to the efficient development and use of information.

2.5 THE CONCEPT OF A PATENT

To organise a market for any commodity it is necessary to have a transferable property right over it. It is useful to distinguish a right of access and a right of exclusion. The former is a right to use an asset, the latter a right to prevent others from using it (except at the holder's discretion). Where non-diffusable assets are concerned the first right necessarily implies the second: to give one person access is to deny it to others. But where a diffusable asset is concerned the capacity of the asset to supply users is theoretically infinite and so the first right does not imply the second. It follows that the right of exclusion must be separately upheld.[4]

Information is a diffusable asset and a legally enforceable right of exclusion over it is known as a patent. Patents can be conferred free of charge, or sold to the highest bidder. The method chosen will govern the distribution of rewards between the patentee and the state.

It was noted in section 2.3 that price discrimination can be implemented in a number of different ways which will give different distributions of market surplus between suppliers and demanders. The simplest method of discrimination is to allow a patentee to fix prices; a profit-maximising patentee will fix them on the basis of the marginal benefit schedule, which means that no surplus at all accrues to consumers. However if patent rights are sold by the state the value of the patent will accrue ultimately to the government, not the patentee, and so a suitable proportion of the surplus can, if desired, be redistributed to consumers through the tax system.

2.6 SALE OF EMBODIED INFORMATION TO FINAL USERS

Although some information may be of intrinsic interest to the consumer, most information is channelled through an intermediate user, and consumed in the form of a product embodying the information, e.g. the consumer purchases a differentiated product designed using marketing information, or a product is produced using an advanced technology.

Four stages in the development and use of information are shown schematically in Figure 2.3, beginning with the formulation of an R and D project and culminating in the consumption of a differentiated or high-technology product. The figure shows how successive stages are connected by markets in different types of information.

Consumers' demand for embodied information is communicated to the initiator of the development via the intermediate user. Consumer purchases influence a user's valuation of the information, and competitive bidding for licences between rival intermediate users ensures that this value is passed on to the initiator.

Efficiency requires that the intermediate user should obtain a positive share of any market surplus while at the same time the marginal consumer of the embodied information should be charged no more than marginal cost. If production (i.e. the embodiment of the information) takes place under constant or increasing returns to scale then it is necessary for the intermediate user to charge discriminatory prices in order to meet these conditions. Only if there are decreasing returns to scale in production is it possible that a uniform price will be efficient.

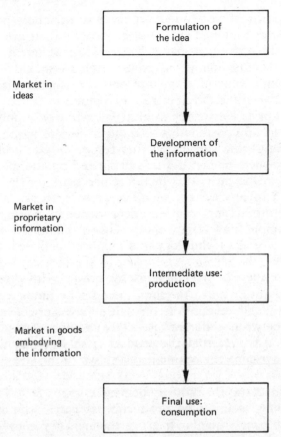

FIGURE 2.3. Four stages in the development and use of information

2.7 LICENSING INFORMATION TO INTERMEDIATE USERS

An item of information may have several intermediate uses, each of which is best exploited by a different user. Or the information may have to be embodied in a good which is optimally produced in several small plants. In either case the proprietor's efficient strategy is to license to several users. But competition between users in exploiting the information may eliminate their private return, and hence the return earned by the proprietor. It is therefore necessary to ensure that intermediate users are coordinated to maintain monopoly power.

Consider first the case of several distinct intermediate uses. We assume that in general each user has some degree of monopoly or monopsony power. Wherever there is monopoly power, each use should be exploited independently only if there are zero cross-price elasticities of demand between the different uses, and wherever there is monopsony power, each use should be exploited independently only if there are zero cross-price elasticities of supply between the different resource inputs.

If cross-price elasticities in either demand or supply are non-zero, failure to coordinate will result in loss of monopoly rents, either because the surplus accrues respectively to consumers or resource owners or because it is dissipated by intermediate users operating inefficiently. It is therefore necessary for the licensor to draw up a royalty system which corrects for the externalities in private return arising from interdependence in intermediate uses.

An example may clarify these general remarks. Consider the case of licensing a technology to a small competitive industry. We assume that the resources supplied to the industry are perfectly elastic, so there is no monopsony power. However, there is monopoly power up to the limit-price set by the best alternative technology, and because of competition cross-price elasticities of demand between different users are infinite. To simplify the analysis we assume that the product is sold at a uniform price. Factors governing the optimal royalty system may be analysed as follows.

In Figure 2.4(a) the industry demand curve is DD'. Under both old and new technology, production is carried on by a large number of small plants. Initially the industry supply curve is $S_0 S_0'$ and industry output is Z. According to Figure 2.4(b) each plant produces an output Q_0 at the minimum of its average cost curve (AC_0) where the marginal cost curve (MC_0) intersects it. With efficient use of the new technology the competitive industry supply curve shifts down to $S_1 S_1'$, and each plant produces a larger output Q_1 at the minimum of AC_1 where MC_1 intersects it.

Suppose to begin with that the proprietor of the information subcontracts production, acting as a monopolist. His marginal cost curve is $S_1 S_1'$, his marginal revenue curve is $S_0 ABM$, and the profit-maximising strategy is to produce where they intersect, C, giving the same industry output as before.

Now suppose that the same result is required from a royalty system. We assume that in licensing the technology to each plant no direct restriction can be imposed on its price or output; control over these variables must be built into the royalty system.

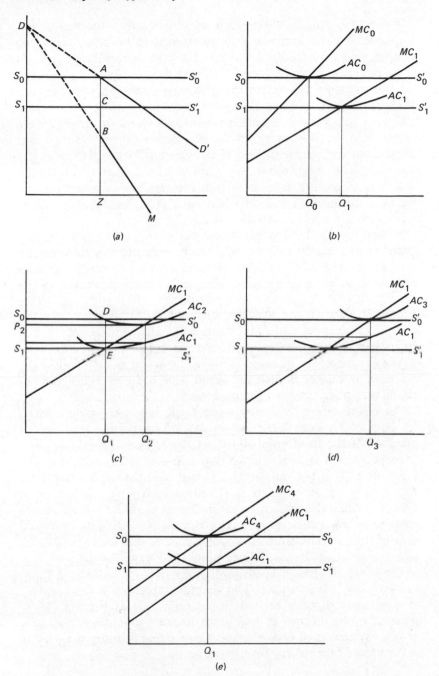

FIGURE 2.4. Royalty systems in a small competitive industry

It is readily established that a lump sum royalty is unsatisfactory. Suppose that the licensor requires from each plant a total lump sum payment, S_0DES_1, equal to his previous monopoly profit from the plant (Figure 2.4(c)). Because fixed lump sum payments do not influence the firm's marginal costs, competition between licensees will drive down the price to P_2, at which level marginal cost is equal to the average cost gross of royalty (as given by the curve AC_2). Each licensee produces a larger output, Q_2, so that there are fewer licensees, and when aggregated over plants royalty payment is less than monopoly profit for the industry as a whole. The loss of profit arises both from the lower price and from the waste of resources incurred when each plant produces at above minimum average cost (net of royalty).

Assuming that the marginal cost curve MC_1 rises more steeply than the average cost curve AC_1, the best that the proprietor can do with a lump sum royalty is to increase the payment to give an average cost curve gross of royalty, AC_3, which is tangent to the supply curve S_0S_0' at the intersection of MC_1 and S_0S_0' (see Figure 2.4(d)). Consumers are charged the limit-price, average cost of production and plant output are higher than before, but price has risen by more than average cost of production and royalty is therefore increased. From the social point of view the waste of resources is also increased, this being a component of the higher price charged to consumers.

An efficient royalty system necessarily has a payment related to output. To encourage profit-maximising plant managers to produce at the minimum of AC_1 it is necessary to adjust their perception of marginal cost so that marginal cost is equal to the limit-price S_0 at the output Q . It is thus necessary to impose a royalty on the marginal unit Q_1 equal to S_0-S_1. At the same time, to obtain the maximum total royalty payment it is necessary that on average the same royalty is paid on each intramarginal unit of output. The simplest royalty system with these properties is a *pro rata* royalty S_0-S_1 per unit (see Figure 2.4(e)).

We conclude that in licensing to a competitive industry a lump sum royalty is inadequate. The simplest satisfactory arrangement is a payment directly related to the output of each plant. More generally, our discussion highlights the fact that the design of a royalty system is of crucial importance in maximising the private return from proprietary information.

2.8   INITIATING THE DEVELOPMENT OF INFORMATION

Suppose that the initial idea for developing the information has been formulated and has been widely diffused. For market forces to be efficient they must ensure that development of the information is not wastefully replicated, and that the developer uses the minimum cost technique for development. When the cost of communicating information is negligible, all replication of the development of information is inefficient.

It can be shown that market forces will normally achieve efficiency only if there is patent protection, not just for the information generated by the development, but for the initial idea itself, as given, say, by an outline programme of research.

Suppose to begin with that there is no patent protection for the programme of research; patent protection is only conferred when development is complete, and is awarded to the first successful developer.

Let development be a stochastic process in which each developer beginning at a given time has the same fixed probability of obtaining the patent right; then in the absence of patent protection for the programme of research, competition between rival developers will induce replication of development up to the point where the number of developers is so high, and the probability of success so low, that the expected return (net of risk premium) faced by an additional developer is less than the cost of development.

Now let development be non-stochastic, but with a trade-off between the time taken over development and the resource costs incurred (see Figure 2.5). By speeding up development using a larger team of workers for a shorter time diseconomies of large-scale organisation are incurred, so that the present value of resource costs rises at an increasing rate as the time taken over development decreases (as shown by the schedule CC'). By bringing forward the date of completion of development the present value of revenues is also increased, but more slowly than costs (as shown by the schedule RR'). The efficient strategy is for the time taken over development to be set at T_0, where the marginal present value of cost equals the marginal present value of revenue.[5] However, in order to deter a competitor who could profit by replicating the development marginally faster so as to pre-empt the patent rights it is necessary instead to set the time taken so

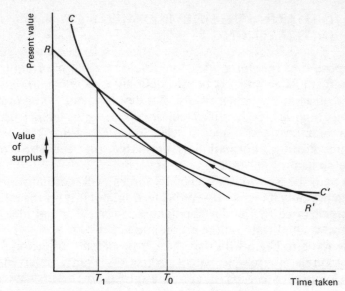

FIGURE 2.5. Optimal development strategy

that the net present value is zero, i.e. to set the time taken to T_1. Thus the whole of the surplus of the development is absorbed by the additional resource costs of fast development.

In the first case the surplus associated with the development is absorbed by wasteful replication and in the second case by wasteful speeding up to deter pre-emption of the patent.

Suppose now that a patent is available for the development programme. The patent may be conferred on the first person to apply with the intention of undertaking the development, or may be auctioned off to the highest bidder. Development will be undertaken if and only if the surplus associated with the patent is non-negative. The patent ensures that there is no replication of development, and thereby allows the successful developer to undertake development using the optimal length of time, T_0.[6]

3 The rationale of the multinational enterprise

3.1 THE CONCEPT OF INTERNALISATION

This chapter considers the extent to which the competitiveness and profitability of the MNE stem from its ability to enhance the efficiency of world-wide resource allocation. It is argued that the advantage of the MNE is based on its facility for transferring resources internationally without exchange of ownership. [1]

In an economy where most resources are privately owned and most goods are privately consumed it is inevitable that specialisation of production will involve exchange of ownership between households through transactions in factor and final product markets. However there are many intermediate products which pass directly between production activities, bypassing the household sector: tangible products such as semi-processed materials and intangible products such as technical information passed on from R and D to routine production. The firm may be defined as an organisation for allocating intermediate products without exchange of ownership; on this view the rationale for the firm rests on the avoidable costs of exchanging ownership when allocating intermediate products. It is argued that these costs are likely to be greatest for certain types of intermediate product, notably for information. It is for this reason that the firm is a major instrument for the transfer of information from R and D to production. The multinationality of the firm arises because most information is relevant to world-wide markets and locational factors often dictate that each market should be serviced by its own separate production unit.

When market transactions are effected by exchange of ownership we speak of 'arm's length' transactions in an 'external' market; when ownership does not change we speak of 'notional' transactions in an 'internal' market.

Sections 3.2 – 3.5 consider the potential benefits of internalisa-

45

tion, while sections 3.6 – 3.9 discuss some of the potential costs. The optimal degree of internalisation is determined by the margin at which the costs and benefits of internalisation are equalised. This margin governs the optimal size and structure of the firm. Section 3.10 develops predictions regarding the nature of the markets most prone to internalisation, and the probable degree of monopoly within them.

The theory predicts that the operations of MNEs will be concentrated in particular areas of economic activity. This provides the guidelines for the theory of foreign direct investment developed in Chapter 4.

3.2   THE MARKET-CLEARING MECHANISM

This section considers the gains to internalisation which stem from greater flexibility in market organisation. This greater flexibility is a consequence of the fact that in an external market price is constrained to act both as an allocator of resources and as a distributor of rewards. But in an internal market the distribution of reward is purely notional and so price acts solely as an allocator.

Microeconomic theory tells us that there are several ways of organising market-clearing; prices may or may not be used, if used they may be fixed either by negotiation or arbitration, and they may be uniform or discriminatory.[2]

We shall argue that in external markets prices must be used, they will be fixed by negotiation and under increasing returns to scale must be discriminatory. On the other hand in internal markets prices may or may not be used, they may be fixed either by negotiation or arbitration, and under increasing returns need not be discriminatory. This greater flexibility creates potential gains to internalisation; the exact magnitude of the gains depends on the type of market involved.

It is readily demonstrated that in an external market transactions will be based on a criterion of price, and prices will be fixed by negotiation. For where exchange of ownership is involved it is the terms of the exchange which govern the willingness to transact, so that price is the criterion which determines whether a transaction is undertaken. Each transactor also likes to be free to use his own bargaining power to influence price, and to exploit the competitive forces constraining others by choosing freely with whom he will transact; he is thus unwilling to surrender all control over price to an arbitrator. The only exception occurs where negotiations are liable to be very protracted; for example in bilateral monopoly where price is indeterminate.

It can also be shown that under increasing returns to scale an efficient level of supply will be forthcoming in an external market only when pricing is discriminatory. For given that supply is voluntary, none will be forthcoming unless a non-negative surplus accrues to the supplier, and under increasing returns the uniform market-clearing price is unable to meet this requirement (see section 2.3).

By contrast the internal market imposes no constraints on the choice of market-clearing mechanism. The allocation can be either planned centrally, choosing the quantities transacted through a process of constrained optimisation, or decentralised through a two-stage procedure which determines quantity response to price and then evaluates an equilibrium set of prices. Centralisation incurs additional communication costs and imposes a heavy burden on the single information processor. On the other hand it avoids the iteration of trial prices and the repeated to-and-fro movement of information associated with it. Thus when communication is slow, non-price coordination may permit a faster response to unforeseen changes in the economic environment, and thereby eliminate waste from temporary misallocations of resources.

In an internal market prices may be set either by negotiation between divisions of the enterprise, or by the *fiat* of an internal arbitrator. To achieve a uniform parametric price it is necessary for the negotiators to be well informed about provisional transactions and for each to be heavily constrained by internal competitive pressures. On the other hand the arbitrator can set a uniform parametric price by virtue of his power of *fiat*. To achieve equilibrium the negotiators respond to unsatisfied demand by raising price and respond to unsold supplies by reducing price; the arbitrator follows a similar principle, but bases his price adjustments on the balance of the aggregates of demand and supply. The analysis suggests that the conditions for a uniform parametric equilibrium price are more likely to be satisfied by arbitration than by negotiation. The benefit to the internal market arising from its access to arbitration reflects the difficulty of maintaining atomistic competition within any market – whether internal or external – and also the gain from centralising information about quantity response when adjusting price.

Internal markets have no need of discriminatory pricing, since any loss on supply is simply a charge on overheads which is fully offset by a surplus on demand.

The problems of implementing price discrimination in an external market are threefold.

Firstly, it requires accurate knowledge of each transactor's reservation prices (Reservation demand price corresponds to marginal benefit, as defined in section 2.3, and reservation supply price to marginal cost.) If a transactor is asked about this price there may be either no response or an untruthful response. The analysis of the 'free rider' problem [3] indicates that a transactor who believes that his response will not ultimately influence his opportunity to trade will deliberately understate his reservation demand price and overstate his reservation supply price.

Secondly, the enforcement of price discrimination requires restrictions on resale. Legal restrictions are usually costly to police. Other restrictions, such as differentiation of the product to a degree which makes it non-transferable between users, are usually difficult to enforce without the collaboration of producers of complementary goods.

A third restriction is imposed by public attitudes, reflected in loss of goodwill for the discriminator and in statutory limitations enforced as part of government competition policy.

To a certain extent the problems of discrimination are more severe in final product markets than in intermediate product markets. Nevertheless the avoidance of price discrimination must rank as a major advantage of internal markets.

3.3 CONTRACTUAL COSTS

In an external market exchange of ownership is organised through a system of contracts. Each party stands to gain if he can default on his obligations (while ensuring that the other party honours the contract) or if he can exploit loopholes to limit his obligations to less than was anticipated by the other party. [4] By contrast in an internal market none of the transactors has any incentive to benefit himself at the expense of others.

The incentive to default in an external market depends upon the anticipated penalty and the probability of detection.[5] In practice the penalties for default tend to be low and in cases of limited liability or bankruptcy may be negligible. If the probability of detection is also low then transactions will tend to break down and efficient allocation will be inhibited. On the other hand if additional resources are devoted to detection the unit costs of policing transactions rise and although fewer transactions break down, fewer are initiated.

In practice a major factor governing the risk of default is the time horizon of the contract. If the contract is spot and effected cash on delivery then the only risk arises from deliberate misrepresentation of product quality, and this can usually be dealt with by testing on the spot a sample of the product. But when the contract is a future one there is a chance that one or other of the parties will be unable to meet his obligations because of bankruptcy or liquidation in the intervening period. Even though nothing may have changed hands the other party may suffer if he has relied on the contract being completed. Similarly if transactions – spot or future – are not effected cash on delivery there is a much greater opportunity for the initial recipient, of either goods or money, to default. Thus in so far as contracts are future rather than spot, and involve pre- or post-payment, the costs of the external market tend to increase.

Loopholes in the drafting of a contract usually arise because the contract fails to cover certain contingencies. These contingencies may be foreseen by one of the parties, who may contrive to induce the contingent events in order to limit his obligations. The problem can be avoided if both parties are sufficiently skilful to foresee all contingencies and build into the contract a system of contingent compensations. The cost of formulating the contract may be quite high, but in most instances will be outweighed by the benefits of mutual insurance.

The cost of closing loopholes will depend on the number of contingencies and this in turn will reflect the complexity of the product and the variety of its uses. Transactions involving sophisticated products may prove very costly to organise in external markets.

3.4   INADEQUATE PROPERTY RIGHTS

This section considers difficulties created by the right of ownership itself rather than difficulties with contracts. The existence of a contract presupposes the existence of a transferable property right, but in practice the property right, or its transferability, may not be well founded in law.

Rights of ownership are frequently ill-defined and difficult to enforce. There is often controversy over whether certain types of good are appropriable for private use. Physical possession is usually taken as *prima facie* evidence of ownership but can always be challenged. To publicise possession is often to invite harmful imitation or replication, or encourage rival claims upon the good. In such cases the best way to maintain possession is through secrecy.

When marketing a good in which ownership is maintained through secrecy there is clearly a dilemma: to sell the good in an external market it is necessary to publicise it, but the consequence of publicity may be that ownership is lost. There are two ways of resolving the problem. The first is to market the good without divulging its precise specification, but to offer the buyer insurance regarding the value of the good; this strategy is discussed further in section 6.2. The second is for the owner of the good to integrate forward into the use of the good and so internalise the market. The main argument against the first strategy is that the sale of insurance involves a contingent futures contract, and therefore encounters the contractual costs discussed in the previous section. Because of this, defects in the system of property rights may well create an incentive to internalise.

In some cases property rights may be well-defined but non-transferable, e.g. certain types of charter or licence. In this event utilisation of an external market is out of the question and the only way to widen exploitation of the right is through internalisation.

3.5   COSTS OF INTERVENTION

Government intervention in markets is often based on price, either directly as with statutory price controls, or indirectly as when tariffs are levied *ad valorem*. In each case there is a potential gain to the private sector from dichotomising real and nominal prices, the real prices being used to guide resource allocation, the nominal prices to present a facade of compliance with price control or to minimise tariff liabilities. Whether social gain or loss results from minimising the incidence of intervention depends upon whether the intervention distorts resource allocation or corrects for externalities elsewhere in the system.

The divorce of real and nominal prices is difficult to achieve in an external market. The problem is to modify the initial distribution of income created by trading at the nominal prices. It would be necessary to associate with each transaction some other transaction in a notional commodity – such as vaguely specified service not actually rendered – the payment for which would make up the balance between the real and nominal price. However, since the second part of the contract, being expressly designed to evade government intervention, would be difficult to enforce in law, the risk of default on this part of the contract would be high. By contrast in an internal market the distribution of income is of no real consequence, so that a nominal transaction is not required; and even if it were needed there would be no risk of default.

Other forms of government intervention can be mitigated by the use of nominal prices. One example is the evasion of controls on international capital movements; the object is to achieve a real transfer of capital while restricting the nominal transfer to zero. Another example is the minimisation of world-wide tax liability when effective rates of tax differ between fiscal areas; the objective here is to achieve a nominal redistribution of income to the low-tax country whilst leaving the real distribution of income unchanged. [6]

In these cases the nominal prices are not used at the point of intervention, but in international product markets. In the first case the strategy is to over-invoice imports into the country restricting outward capital movement, and in the second case to over-invoice exports from the country with the lowest effective rate of tax. As before, over-invoicing in an external market involves a significant risk of default, which is avoided by an internal market. The use of nominal prices in this way is known as 'transfer pricing'.

3.6 THE PROBLEM OF INCENTIVE

It was noted in section 3.2 that external markets determine the
distribution of rewards between transactors but internal markets
do not. A corollary of this is that in an external market an
individual who improves his effort or efficiency is rewarded
directly through the market mechanism. On the other hand in an
internal market the individual transactor is normally a delegate
of the internaliser, e.g. a manager of one of the divisions of the
enterprise. An increase in his personal efficiency rewards the
internaliser rather than himself, so that there is no incentive for
efficient individual performance.

Such lack of incentive creates a risk of default in the supply of
managerial service – managers will tend to pursue their own
objectives rather than those of their employer. To meet this
problem the internaliser must invest resources in monitoring
managerial performance, and reward employees on the basis of
measured efficiency. [7]

In effect internalisation translates the risk of default from the
intermediate product market to the market for managerial services
to administer product allocation. Thus while contractual costs
in the product market are reduced by internalisation, contractual
costs elsewhere tend to be increased.

3.7 COSTS OF MARKET FRAGMENTATION

The effect of internalisation is often to fragment the intermediate
product market: a unified well-integrated world market is split
into a number of smaller markets operated by different firms.
There are two reasons why this may reduce efficiency.

Firstly there may be increasing returns to scale in the market-
clearing system. The typical system involves an infrastructure of
channels of communication (post, telephones, etc) connecting
administrative units which collect information, process it and
store it. Although the infrastructure typically exhibits increasing
returns it can normally be shared with other users, and so does
not influence the optimum size of the market-clearing system (e.g.
post and telephone services are hired at uniform parametric
prices). On the other hand, while administrative units exhibit
fewer cases of increasing returns, they are less easy to share with

other users. Information storage systems, and processing units which require limited inputs of specialised skills, often exhibit increasing returns. In such cases the optimal scale of an internal market is likely to be fairly large, and consequently for a small intermediate product market the optimal degree of fragmentation is likely to be very low.

The second issue depends upon whether the internal market is open or closed. A market is open if transactions with outside parties are permitted, and is closed if they are not. If an internal market is closed its optimal scale is likely to be very much larger than if it were open. When a market is closed it is necessary to match the scales of the supplying activity and the demanding activity through the internal market alone. It is well known that when the minimum efficient scale of the supplying activity is x and the minimum efficient scale of the demanding activity is y then the minimum efficient scale of the intermediate product market is the lowest common multiple of x and y, which may be many times larger than either x or y. When the internal market is closed this constitutes its minimum efficient scale, whereas when the market is open no such constraint applies.

3.8 THE PROBLEM OF DIVERSITY

Under internalisation quite distinct activities are brought under common ownership and control. The internaliser of a single market operates both the activity which constitutes the source of demand and the activity which constitutes the source of supply. If a whole chain of markets is internalised, as may sometimes occur in a multi-stage production sequence, the internaliser may be responsible for a large number of separate activities.

The internaliser must have access to the technical know-how to operate all these activities. Either he has wide-ranging expertise himself, or he is able to hire the expertise. In practice it is usually beyond the powers of any one person to master the technical details of several distinct activities. But if he is obliged to hire the expertise it is necessary for him to have sufficient background knowledge to understand the scope and limitations of the expertise required, and to have means of screening for the integrity and ability of those offering to supply it. This in turn requires diverse knowledge of a rather more general kind.

An internaliser without this diverse knowledge would be exposed to risks arising from his inability to value accurately the expertise supplied to him. It is not sufficient for an internaliser to recognise the potential gains from internalisation. He must also have the ability to hire at competitive rates the skills to which other firms, specialised in just one activity, have access. Similarly, if he were to internalise by merging existing going concerns, he must value accurately each of the firms he intends to take over. If he undervalues his bid will be unsuccessful, while if he over-values the integrated firm will be burdened with losses arising from excessive payments to former proprietors.

It can be argued that the broad-based knowledge necessary for successful internalisation is one of the scarcest types of managerial expertise. It is so much a reflection of an individual's social background, education and business experience that it may be regarded as a quasi-fixed factor. As such the limited endowment of this factor must be regarded as a major constraint on the growth of internal markets, and hence a major factor influencing the size of the integrated firm.

If the successful internaliser is someone who synthesises knowledge from diverse sources then the ease with which the relevant knowledge can be synthesised will influence the degree of internalisation. When the internal market spans the boundaries of very different societies, cultures and languages, it will be difficult for anyone to synthesise the relevant commercial know-ledge, and hence the probability of successful internalisation is very low. Similarly if personal transportation and other forms of communication are difficult, synthesis is less likely, if only because it is more costly to achieve. Thus the extent to which internalisation is constrained by the diversity of knowledge required of the interaliser will reflect the spatial characteristics of the market, and in particular the extent of social, cultural, linguistic and geo-graphical barriers to communication.

3.9 THE PROBLEMS OF FOREIGN OWNERSHIP

An internaliser of an international market will normally have the status of foreign owner in one or more of the locations in which he operates. The only exception concerns companies registered with multiple nationality and operating only in countries in which they are registered.

Foreign owners are often discriminated against. Their assets are susceptible to expropriation, often with inadequate compensation. Also customers tend to favour indigenous firms; in particular the host government may discriminate against foreign firms when awarding contracts in strategic areas such as defence. The extent of discrimination tends to reflect the state of political relations between source and host countries. When the two countries belong to different spheres of political or military influence the risks of foreign ownership may be a significant deterrent to internalisation.

3.10 THE COSTS AND BENEFITS OF INTERNALISATION

Profit-maximising firms will internalise markets up to the margin where the private benefit is equal to the private cost. By comparing the costs and benefits of internalisation discussed in the previous sections this result should predict those markets which are most susceptible to internalisation.

The preceding analysis is summarised in Tables 3.1 and 3.2, which classify respectively the benefits and costs of internalisation. Each table gives examples of the types of market failure which influence internalisation, and compares the internal and external solutions in each case. It is useful to classify these factors according to whether they reflect the nature of the industry in which the product is traded, or the nature of the locations between which it is traded.

The analysis suggests two types of industry in which internalisation will predominate. The first is industries which rely heavily on proprietary information, the second industries which operate multi-stage production processes under increasing returns to scale or with capital-intensive techniques.

There are three main factors which encourage the internalisation of proprietary information. Firstly, because of inadequacies in the patent system property rights in information are insecure and therefore often need to be maintained through secrecy; this creates the problem of 'buyer uncertainty'. Secondly, there is the problem of enforcing price discrimination. Finally, the complexity of the uses of information makes it easy for contractual loopholes to occur in licensing arrangements.

Internalisation of information flow leads to the integration of R and D with production. In this context R and D is a broad

TABLE 3.1. Classification of gains from internalisation

Problem that creates incentive to internalise	Example	External solution	Internal solution	Specificity of problem
1. Costs of market clearing				
1.1. Decentralisation of decision-taking	Sluggish price adjustment to unforeseen change	None	Use centralised non-price planning	Industry – specific
1.2. Need for negotiation	(i) Costs of sanctions enforced as part of bargaining strategy in bilateral monopoly	None	Replace bargaining by arbitrator's *fiat*	Industry – specific
	(ii) Time costs of continually renegotiating short-term contracts with the same individual in a fluctuating market	Use long-term contracts (but see 2.1(i))	As above	Industry – specific
1.3. Implementing price discrimination	(i) Preventing resale	Differentiate product to make it non-transferable between uses	Discrimination unnecessary: charge all users at marginal cost and impute the loss of overheads	Industry – specific

(ii) Meeting government competition policy and avoiding loss of goodwill	None	As above	Industry – specific
(iii) 'Free rider' problem in determining reservation prices	None	As above	Industry – specific
2. Contractual costs **2.1. Default** (i) Debtor goes bankrupt or invokes limited liability	None	No incentive to default	General
(ii) Failure to honour futures contract, for reasons excluded from 2.1(i)	Write penalties into contract. Acquire sanctions sufficient to enforce payment of penalty (e.g. make other party accept trade credit)	As above	Industry – specific
(iii) Misrepresentation of quantity or quality	Both buyer and seller measure quantity and check quality	No incentive to misrepresent: Duplication of effort unnecessary	General

TABLE 3.1. (*continued*)

Problem that creates incentive to internalise	Example	External solution	Internal solution	Specificity of problem
2.2. Contractual loopholes	Failure of contract to cover some contingency	Invest additional effort in formulating the contract	No incentive to exploit loopholes	Industry – specific
3. Costs of inadequate property rights	(i) Maintaining secrecy when title to commodity is insecure creates 'buyer uncertainty'	Specify commodity vaguely but offer to insure the buyer	Confidentiality is maintained	Industry – specific
	(ii) Property right held is not legally transferable	None	Transfer unnecessary	Industry – specific

4. Costs of intervention

4.1. Price control	Price of intermediate product fixed by statute	Arrange to invoice at nominal price but with redistribution of income through notional transaction (but see 2.1(i) and 2.2)	Invoice at nominal price: no redistribution necessary	Industry – specific
4.2. Tariffs	*Ad valorem* tariff levied on imports, or *ad valorem* tax on exports	As above	As above	Customs boundary – specific
4.3. Differential international taxation	Rates of corporate income tax differ between countries	Similar to above	Similar to above	Fiscal boundary – specific
4.4. Quotas on capital movements	Restrictions on outward capital movements	Similar to above	Similar to above	Currency boundary – specific

TABLE 3.2. Classification of costs of internalisation

Nature of cost	Example	Internal solution	External solution	Specificity of problem
1. Loss of managerial incentive	Administrators of market-clearing work leisurely	Monitor administrators, use incentive payments, promotion and demotion	Each transactor has strong incentive	General
2. Cost of market fragmentation	(i) Indivisible resources in market-clearing are under-utilised.	None	No fragmentation	General
	(ii) Individual activities have to operate at less than minimum efficient scale	'Open up' internal market	As above	Industry – specific
3. Cost of acquiring diverse information	Formation of internal market involves acquisition and operation of diverse activities	None	Acquisition of information unnecessary	Geographical, social and linguistic boundary – specific
4. Risk of expropriation	Host country does not respect property right in plant and equipment	None	No foreign ownership of plant and equipment	Political boundary – specific

concept which includes the development of marketing skills and management systems as well as the development of technology. When the information is relevant to the production of goods for a world-wide market it is quite likely, given the impact of trade barriers such as tariffs and transport costs, that the optimal strategy will be to service the world market through multi-plant production. In this case the firm becomes horizontally integrated with plants producing the same product in different locations. When the locations span national boundaries the result is an MNE.

Consider now the case of an intermediate product market in multi-stage production. If there are increasing returns to scale in one or more of the stages then price discrimination will be necessary in an external market; furthermore if two adjacent stages exhibit increasing returns then bilateral monopoly may emerge, with its associated negotiation costs. Secondly, if there are significant production lags, or if durable goods are extensively used, then efficient intertemporal coordination will call for a futures market in the intermediate good; a spot market is sufficient for coordination only in the steady state. But futures contracts in an external market involve substantial risks of default. Since production lags and the use of durable equipment are both reflected in the capital-intensity of production, the higher the capital-intensity the greater will be the difficulty of organising an efficient external market for the intermediate product. This suggests that when multi-stage production is associated with increasing returns to scale or high capital intensity there will be a strong incentive to internalise.

Internalisation of an intermediate product market generates vertical integration. When factor prices differ between locations and barriers to trade are relatively low there is normally an incentive to base different stages of production at different locations, so as to match factor intensity at each stage to factor abundance. When the locations are in different countries vertical integration creates an MNE.

Locational factors also influence the incentive to internalise. Internalisation will predominate in markets where there are opportunities for transfer pricing, i.e. markets which span the boundaries of customs, fiscal and currency areas, and will be greater the higher the tariffs, the larger the tax differentials between the fiscal areas and the more severe the restrictions on capital movements between the currency areas. Internalisation will be least in markets which span areas where there are significant differences in social structure, culture and language, or where the countries concerned are politically hostile.

The degree to which internalisation fragments the market depends mainly on the nature of the product. Information being indivisible, a market in information cannot be fragmented so long as the information remains proprietary and not public. However it is possible for several firms to be involved in exploiting similar, closely substitutable, items of proprietary information. The fragmentation of an intermediate product market in multi-stage production depends largely on the lowest common multiple of the minimum efficient scales of plant. If this is large relative to total market size then few firms will be involved, while if the lowest common denominator is relatively small then a large number of firms may be involved.

Finally, it should be noted that the balance between the costs and benefits of internalisation determines not only the type of market which is internalised, but also the optimal size and structure of the firm. However the application of the theory of internalisation to this particular issue is behond the scope of this book.

4 A theory of foreign direct investment, technology transfer, trade and capital movements

4.1 INTRODUCTION

This chapter considers the role of MNEs in trade and capital movements. The analysis is based on very strong assumptions which are equivalent to ignoring the potential social costs of MNEs. The emphasis is much more on the fact that in an imperfect world the creation of an MNE may under certain conditions improve efficiency. The analysis demonstrates, firstly, that under certain conditions an MNE's location of production is similar to that generated by international competition between purely national firms and, secondly, that foreign direct investment flows owe little or nothing to international differences in capital endowments, and almost everything to the economics of horizontal and vertical integration in specific industries. The analysis constitutes an extension and application of the Heckscher-Ohlin (HO) model of trade. Non-specialist readers, or those mainly interested in applications, may prefer to omit this chapter on a first reading.

4.2 THE HECKSCHER-OHLIN MODEL

The simplest variant of the HO model assumes two countries, two commodities and two factors of production. Each commodity is produced by combining the two factors of production, with diminishing marginal returns to each factor and constant returns to scale. The technology of production is the same in each country. Both commodities are tradeable with negligible transport costs. On the other hand the factors are immobile between countries, although perfectly mobile between industries within the same country. The two factors are usually distinguished as labour and

63

capital; units of each factor are perfectly homogeneous and infinitely divisible. Each country has a fixed endowment of each factor.

The capital intensity of an industry is defined as the ratio of capital to labour used in that industry; it is assumed that the marginal rate of substitution of capital for labour increases as capital intensity increases. There is said to be factor intensity regularity between two industries if for any given marginal rate of substitution the capital intensity in one industry is always higher than in the other. A country is incompletely specialised if it produces some of each commodity. Using these concepts we can state two major results of the HO model.

The Heckscher-Ohlin theorem asserts that with factor intensity regularity and incomplete specialisation it is efficient for countries to trade so that each country exports the commodity which uses most intensively the factor in which the country is relatively most abundant. The factor-price equalisation theorem asserts that under the same conditions the efficient pattern of trade equalises the prices of each factor in the two countries. A corollary of this is that trade in commodities is a perfect substitute for movement of factors: when trade equalises factor prices there are no further welfare gains available from factors being mobile.

It must be admitted that the assumptions of the HO model are very strict. The results of the model are sensitive to the assumptions of identical technology in each country and constant returns to scale. However the restrictions on the numbers of countries, commodities and factors are not always essential in that the results of the simple model generalise when they are relaxed. For example it can be shown that under certain conditions factor prices in two countries will be equalised by trade provided that the number of tradeable commodities is no less than the number of immobile factors.

The assumptions regarding labour and capital are particularly strict. Few real world factors are immobile between countries yet perfectly mobile between industries. Furthermore it is unusual for real world capital goods to be mobile between industries yet completely inelastic in total supply. Thus while the HO model provides some very strong results characterising the efficient international allocation of resources, the assumptions of the model limit its applicability. Unfortunately it is outside the scope of this book to develop an alternative to the HO model.

4.3 INTERNALISATION AND EFFICIENCY

Although the rationale of internalisation is market failure, it can be shown that, given two key conditions, the behaviour of internal markets will be efficient.

Firstly, recall from Chapter 3 that the private gain from internalisation stems mainly from the appropriation of an increase in social welfare due to the avoidance of external market imperfections. Suppose that this is the sole source of gains from internalisation. Then the gain from internalisation is equal to the increase in market surplus, and since the increase in surplus is positive only if efficiency is improved, internalisation will take place if and only if it enhances efficiency. To put it another way, when competitive forces act to seek out the most profitable form of market organisation, the most profitable form will be the most efficient form, so that internal or external markets will be selected depending on which is the most efficient.

Secondly, suppose that of all possible market organisations the most efficient one is also perfectly efficient. Thus while different market organisations have different costs of operation, and comparison of these costs determines the chosen organisation, the chosen organisation will necessarily be efficient.

These two conditions together imply that when internalisation occurs it is the most efficient organisation and, being the most efficient organisation, is perfectly efficient. Thus although internalisation occurs because of market imperfections, internal markets themselves are perfectly efficient.

The limitations of the two conditions are examined in the next chapter, as part of a more general inquiry into the social costs and benefits of internalisation.

4.4 VERTICAL INTEGRATION IN THE HECKSCHER-OHLIN MODEL

If an internal market is efficient then the associated pattern of trade and capital movements can be predicted using the HO theory.

The simplest form of internalisation to analyse is that associated with vertical integration. Suppose there is a single consumer good which is produced in two stages. The first stage produces an intermediate product, which is input to the second stage to produce the final product.[1] If a fixed input of the intermediate product is used per unit output of the final product then in effect there is joint consumption of the first-stage product and the second-stage product.

If the intermediate product market is externalised there will be no MNEs, but if it is internalised all international trade will be carried out by MNEs. The role of MNEs in world trade may be derived diagrammatically; the derivation has three stages.

The first stage determines the production strategy for the world economy. In Figure 4.1 units of labour are measured horizontally and units of capital vertically. $AD = BC$ is the world endowment of labour and $AB = CD$ the world endowment of capital. Inputs of factors to the first stage of production are measured from the origin A and inputs to the second stage are measured from the origin B. Any point in the box represents a specific allocation of factors between the two stages of production. Emanating from the origin A is an 'isoquant map' showing the various minimal combinations of inputs needed to produce given amounts of output from the first stage of production. The map is drawn assuming that specialisation is incomplete, so that the same factor proportions are used in each country. A similar isoquant map for the second stage of production emanates from the origin B. Efficiency in factor allocation is achieved only at a point of tangency between

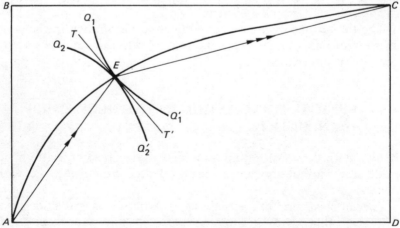

FIGURE 4.1. Efficient production in a Hecksher–Ohlin model

two isoquants; the locus of such points is the production contract curve *AEC*. However only one point on this curve is compatible with the restriction that first- and second-stage production be undertaken in fixed proportion; in the figure this point, denoted *E*, is at the tangency of the isoquants Q_1EQ_1' and Q_2EQ_2' . The slope of the ray *AE* measures the capital intensity of the first stage of production; the slope of the ray *CE* the capital intensity of the second stage of production.

The second part of the analysis determines the consumption strategy for the world economy. The distribution of consumption between countries is governed by the international distribution of income. Following the neoclassical theory we shall assume that the factor prices associated with the efficient production strategy are the basis for the functional distribution of income. Applying these prices to the international factor endowments determines the international distribution of income. The constraint that consumer expenditure cannot exceed income thence determines the pattern of consumption.

The dimensions of the box in Figure 4.2 are similar to those in Figure 4.1 but the interpretation of the axes is different. Instead of measuring the allocation of factors to stages of production we now measure the allocation of factors to countries; the allocation to country 1 is measured from the origin *A* and the allocation to country 2 from the origin *C*. The international endowment of

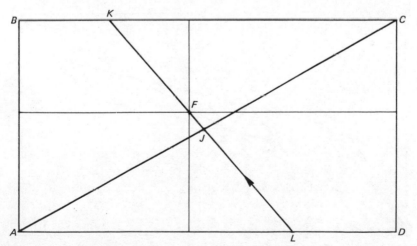

FIGURE 4.2. Determination of consumption in a Heckscher–Ohlin model

factors is fixed at *F*. Relative factor prices are determined by the slope of the tangent *TET ′*. We define a country's 'command' over a factor as the quantity of the factor used indirectly to satisfy consumer wants in that country. By drawing a line *KFL* parallel to *TET ′* through *F* we obtain a locus of international distribution of factor command. Any point on this line shows a particular allocation of factors to satisfying consumer wants in each country compatible with each country's income from factor ownership. But only one point on this line is compatible with the restriction to joint consumption, for with joint consumption the same proportion of both factors must be allocated to servicing consumption in each country; hence consumption strategy is restricted to the diagonal *AJC*. The restrictions imposed by income distribution and joint consumption therefore determine a unique allocation of factors to consumption, represented by the point *J* at the intersection of *KFL* and *AJC*.

The third stage of the analysis compares production and consumption strategies to determine the pattern of trade. The method is to express factor endowments and factor commands in terms of the activity levels of each stage of production. This translation is effected in Figure 4.3, in which the axes and labels are similar to those of Figure 4.2. Each ray represents the utilisation of factors at a particular stage of production; the intensities with which factors are used at each stage are determined from the

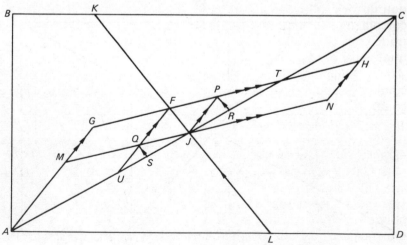

FIGURE 4.3. Trade flows in a Heckscher—Ohlin model

rays *AE* and *CE* in Figure 4.1. The figure shows that *AG* units of the first-stage output are produced in country 1 and *CH* units in country 2; *GF* units of the second-stage output are produced in country 1 and *HF* units in country 2. *AM* units of the first stage output are consumed in country 1 and *CN* units in country 2; *MJ* units of the second-stage output are consumed in country 1 and *NJ* units in country 2. Comparison of consumption and production shows that *GM=QF* units of the first-stage output are exported from country 1 in return for imports from country 2 of *FP=QJ* units of the second-stage output.

Under internalisation each firm controls both stages of production and operates each stage at a level which is compatible with the internal supply or demand of the other stage. When internal trade spans national boundaries an MNE is created. According to the figure MNEs are responsible for the export from country 1 of *QF=JP* units of the first-stage output, and also for the production of *PT* units of the second-stage output in country 2 which are combined with it. MNEs are also responsible for the export from country 2 of *FP=QJ* units of the second-stage output, and also for the production of *QU* units of first-stage output in country 1 which are combined with it. If these flows are valued using equilibrium factor prices then MNEs in country 1 produce *US* units of first-stage output for domestic consumption (when combined with imported second-stage output) and *SJ* units for export; MNEs in country 2 produce *JR* units of second-stage output for export and *RT* units for domestic consumption (when combined with imported first-stage output). The total value of trade [2] (all of which is undertaken by MNEs) is *SR=2SJ* and the total value of MNE output is *UT*. Of the remaining world output, *AU* is generated by uninational vertically integrated firms in country 1 and *TC* by uninational vertically integrated firms in country 2.

4.5 HORIZONTAL INTEGRATION IN THE HECKSCHER-OHLIN MODEL

Internalisation of markets in proprietary information generates horizontal integration. An efficient internal market makes the information available for all uses in which its value exceeds the marginal cost of communication. If communication costs are negligible then the proprietary information will be diffused internationally to all industries where it is relevant. The diffusion is channelled through the foreign subsidiaries of the MNE. As a consequence the HO assumption that all countries have access to the same technology remains valid. However through discriminatory pricing the proprietor of the information is able to appropriate all of the quasi-rent attributable to the information; hence there is net transfer of income to the proprietor equal to the excess of the value of the information over its cost of development. Thus the usual HO analysis must be modified to take account of the redistribution of income associated with the transfer of technology. Subject to this qualification the HO theory should predict the trade pattern which emerges as a result of technology transfer by the MNE. [3]

If certain simplifying assumptions are made the trade pattern may be solved geometrically. Let us retain the assumption of joint consumption made in the previous section and in addition assume that the costs of both developing and communicating the information are negligible. Suppose that there is a marginal Hicks-neutral technical improvement [4] in the first stage of production; the relevant isoquant map remains unchanged but the isoquants are relabelled so that each now refers to a proportionately higher output. It follows that the contract curve in Figure 4.1 remains unchanged, but the point E no longer represents compatible outputs from the two stages of production. To restore compati-

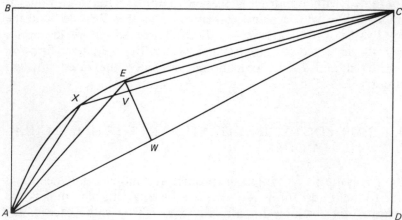

FIGURE 4.4. Hicks-neutral technical progress in a Heckscher–Ohlin model

bility fewer resources must be allocated to the first stage of production, so that E is replaced by a point X on the portion AE of the contract curve (see Figure 4.4). To determine X we use the result that the proportional rate of technical progress in the first stage of production is equal to the proportional increase in world income divided by the proportion of world income generated in the first stage of production. When technical progress is marginal and induces negligible change in relative factor prices the numerator and denominator may be approximated as follows. Draw EVW tangent to the isoquants at E, to intersect CX at V and the diagonal AC at W. Since there is no technical progress in the second stage of production the proportional increase in world income is equal to the proportional increase in factors used in the second stage, which may be measured by XV/CV. At the same time the proportion of world income generated by the first stage of production is AW/AC. Hence the rate of technical progress is equal to $(XV/CV)/(AW/AC)$ which determines X.

Given X, the international consumption pattern is determined by Figure 4.5. In this figure the axes represent the allocation of factors to countries rather than industries. The international distribution of factor command prior to the transfer of income is represented by the line K^1FL^1 drawn through the representative point of factor endowments F parallel to the isoquants at X. The

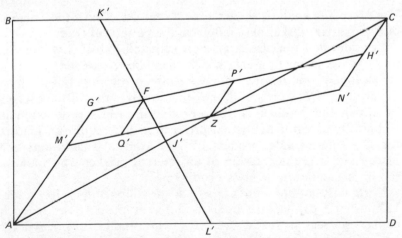

FIGURE 4.5. The income-effect of technology transfer in a Heckscher–Ohlin model

corresponding consumption distribution is determined by the intersection J' of this line with the diagonal AWC. Total quasi-rent attributable to the technology is approximately a proportion XV/XC of world income. The transfer of quasi-rent to the country owning the technology is therefore a proportion XV/XC of the donor country's income. Suppose for example that all shareholders in the technology are nationals of country 1; by appropriating the quasi-rent they induce a repatriation of $J'Z = (XV/XC)J'C$ from country 2. Thus AZ units of final product are consumed in country 1 and CZ units in country 2.

A comparison of the production strategy represented by X with the consumption strategy represented by Z determines the pattern of trade. Under internalisation all of the first stage of production will be controlled by the proprietors of the technology. An MNE controlled from country 1 produces AG' units of first stage output in country 1 and CH' units in country 2; it exports $M'G'$ units from country 1 but nothing from country 2. Country 2 operates a balance of trade surplus, exporting $FP' = Q'Z$ units of second stage product in return for imports of only $M'G'$ units of first stage product. The surplus finances the payment of quasi-rent to the MNE in country 1.

4.6 THE IMPACT OF INTERNALISATION ON TRADE

The preceding analysis suggests two examples of how the creation of an internal market may influence the pattern of trade.

Consider first the case of an intermediate product. Let there be a single consumer good which can be produced by two technologies: one involves a single stage of production in which the product is 'custom-built', the other involves two distinct stages by which the product is 'mass-produced'. Mass production is technically superior to custom production but requires a market for the intermediate product. When external institutions are inadequate it is the creation of an internal market which allows the implementation of mass production.

With custom production there is no opportunity for trade. Labour and capital are used in different proportions in each country (depending on factor endowments) and factor prices differ between countries. Mass production effectively increases the number of commodities from one to two. Under factor intensity regularity the capital-abundant country specialises in the capital-intensive stage of production and the labour-abundant country in the labour-intensive stage of production. Thus the implementation of mass production is spontaneously trade-creating. The impact on factor prices depends on the characteristics of the new technology. If it is capital-intensive then capital rentals will tend to be raised relative to wage rates, although if relative factor endowments differ significantly between countries it may possibly be lowered in the capital-scarce country.

It is often suggested that there is a trend toward standardisation of design and production over the life of a product. In some cases standardisation takes the form of resolving the product into a number of distinct component parts. Our analysis suggests that this tendency will create trade in intermediate products, and as such will serve to equalise factor prices internationally. In so far as intermediate product markets are internalised, the MNE will act as a vehicle for factor price equalisation.

Consider now the creation of an internal market for information. A proprietary technology has been originated in one country and on grounds of comparative advantage the product embodying it should be produced abroad. However the external market for technology does not permit diffusion out of the originating country. For example, because of buyer uncertainty potential licensees in the host country are not only unwilling to pay the full value of the licence but will not even pay an amount equal to the net revenue that the proprietor of the technology can obtain by exporting; hence the proprietor prefers exporting to licensing. However the internal market for technology is costless – by producing abroad and charging discriminatory prices world-wide the proprietor can appropriate the full value of the technology.

Suppose that the technical progress originates in the 'high technology' industry. Prior to internalisation the country originating the technology will *ceteris paribus* have a comparative advantage in producing the high technology good. After internalisation no country has privileged access to technology and comparative advantage is determined solely by relative factor endowments. It follows that the effect of technology transfer is to inhibit imports of the high-technology good into the host country and to substitute for them imports of the good which uses most intensively the source country's relatively most abundant factor. Since the host country has to finance royalty payments through a trade surplus it is likely that its imports will on balance contract.

4.7 THE MacDOUGALL THEORY OF CAPITAL MOVEMENTS

It is customary to analyse capital movements in the context of an HO model in which capital is mobile but labour is not. An obvious starting point is the generalisation of the factor price equalisation theorem referred to in section 4.2. This states that when there are as many goods as factors trade in goods will normally be sufficient to equalise factor prices. Introducing factor mobility under these conditions will not increase efficiency but simply multiply the number of possible trade patterns. To make the analysis determinate it is therefore necessary either to reduce the number of goods to one or to increase the number of factors to three. The first approach is much simpler, and is the one considered here. The second approach is developed in the next section.

Since in each country there is only one industry and a fixed endowment of labour it is possible to derive for each country a schedule showing how the marginal product of capital varies with

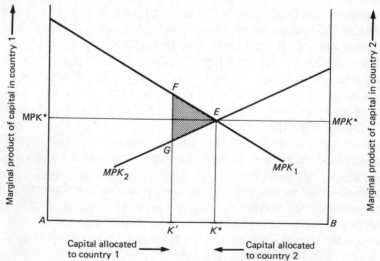

FIGURE 4.6. Efficient capital movement in a two-factor one-commodity world

the quantity of capital allocated to that country. The area under the curve measures the total output of the economy, and the sum of the two areas measures world output. In this simple model efficiency involves maximising world output.

In Figure 4.6 the allocation of capital to country 1 is measured along the horizontal axis from the left-hand origin A and the allocation of capital to country 2 is measured in the reverse direction from the right-hand origin B. The world capital stock is fixed at an amount equal to the distance AB. The schedules of the marginal productivity of capital in the two countries are respectively MPK_1 and MPK_2: both are downward sloping with respect to capital. The schedules intersect at E, which corresponds to an allocation of AK^* units of capital to country 1 and K^*B units of capital to country 2. It is readily established that this allocation is necessary and sufficient for efficiency.

Consider an alternative allocation, say K'. The loss of output in country 1 is given by the area $K'FEK^*$, while the gain in output in country 2 is given by the area $K'GEK^*$. Thus the net loss of output is equal to the area of the shaded triangle EFG. Since the loss is always positive no other allocation can improve upon K^*, and only by setting K' equal to K^* can the loss be reduced to zero.

It is a characteristic of the intersection E that the marginal products of capital are equalised at MPK^*. It follows that the equalisation of marginal products of capital is both necessary and sufficient for the efficient international allocation of capital.

It can also be shown that the efficient allocation will equalise the capital intensities and the wage rates in the two countries.

4.8 CAPITAL MOVEMENTS, TECHNOLOGY TRANSFER AND TRADE

Capital movements are neither a necessary nor sufficient condition for foreign direct investment. They are unnecessary because the purchase of a controlling equity interest in foreign assets can be financed by local borrowing in the host capital market. They are insufficient because loans can be made to finance purchases of foreign assets without any control over the assets being acquired.

There appears to be only one case in which there is a direct link between capital movements and FDI, and even in this case the FDI does not itself constitute the movement of capital. This is the case in which the legitimate productive operations of the MNE are used as a camouflage to bypass statutory restrictions on the movement of capital between currency areas. By over-valuing the sales of a host country division to a source country division funds can be transferred internally by the MNE. Thus when exchange controls are imposed between two currency areas there will be an incentive for investors to direct funds away from strictly financial institutions, such as mutual funds, toward MNEs whose productive activities span the currency areas concerned. In this case the MNE will have an incentive to act as a vehicle for international diversification of individuals' portfolios; its share valuation will be maximised when it locates its investments so that co-variations in profit streams from different sources are minimised. [5]

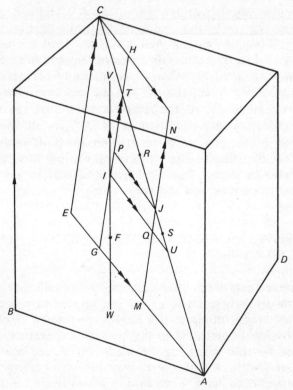

FIGURE 4.7. Trade flows and capital movements in a three-factor two-commodity Heckscher–Ohlin model

However there may be indirect links between capital movements and FDI stemming from the fact that a technology transfer effected by FDI may induce changes in location strategy which influence trade and capital movements. [6]

A simple model of the connection between trade flows and capital movements is presented in Figure 4.7. The model is developed by introducing a mobile factor into the model of section 4.4. Two immobile factors (labour and land) are measured horizontally along the respective axes AB and AD, and the mobile factor (capital) along the vertical axis. If the allocations of factors to industries are measured from the origins A and C then E is the point on the contract curve representing the production of the two commodities in the requisite fixed proportion. The slopes of the rays AE, CE measure the factor proportions of the respective commodities.

We now redefine the axes to represent the allocation of factors by country. The allocation of factors between countries is constrained by the vertical line VW. Given the factor proportions in each industry the only allocation of capital consistent with an efficient production strategy is represented by I. Comparison with the initial allocation represented by F shows that there will be a net export of capital from country 2 equal to FI.

The initial allocation of factors together with relative factor prices determines the international distribution of factor command. Geometrically the distribution is described by a plane (not shown) which is parallel to the tangent at E and passes through F. International consumption strategy is determined by J, the intersection of the plane with the diagonal AJC. Country's 1's consumptions of first- and second-stage output are measured respectively by AM and MJ, while country 2's respective consumptions are measured by CN and NJ.

Comparison of production and consumption strategies shows that country 1's exports of first-stage output are measured by $QI=JP$ and country 2's exports of second-stage output by $QJ=IP$. If the points R and S on the diagonal AJC are of equivalent factor command to P and Q respectively then the value of world trade is RS. The excess of the value of country 1's exports over the value of its imports pays for its acquisition of FI units of capital.

The analysis illustrates the general proposition that factor mobility is trade inhibiting. For example if the two countries differ principally in their capital/labour ratios then capital will be imported into the labour-intensive country to substitute for imports of the capital-intensive good.

Suppose now that there is technical progress in one of the industries. Is there any reason to suppose that the transfer of technology will be accompanied by a transfer of capital as well? Technical progress in capital-intensive industries is not normally sufficient to produce this effect, for the technology will be transferred to capital-abundant countries which will tend to export rather than import capital.

On the other hand the development of technology is a time-consuming process and so is itself a capital-intensive activity. It will therefore tend to be located in capital-abundant countries, which will this export both technology and capital. But perhaps the most important consideration is that technical progress tends to be focused on growth industries, so that any country with a comparative advantage in a growth industry will not only import technology but also import capital to alleviate increasing factor scarcity. If the technical progress is the cause of the growth of the industry then the movements of technology and capital may be closely linked. As we have seen, however, this link owes nothing to any fundamental complementarity between source country technology and source country capital.

4.9 LIMITATIONS OF THE THEORY, AND IMPLICATIONS FOR FUTURE RESEARCH

Our analysis has shown how an integrated theory of trade, technology transfer and capital movements can be synthesised from the theory of market failure and the theory of efficient markets. Reconciliation of the theories is possible because market failure is a property of a particular institutional arrangement; so long as there are several possible institutional arrangements for a given market, failure of one arrangement is compatible with efficient organisation of the market as a whole.

We have focused on a very simple case where there are no taxes or tariffs, constant returns to scale and incomplete specialisation. In this case the theory of efficient markets predicts that MNEs' location and choice of technique will follow the HO theory and their financing the MacDougall theory. These predictions are not refuted by recent MNE behaviour, although two important qualifications must be noted. The first is that the theory does not apply to the era of the 'technology gap', which may be regarded as a transitional phase before the MNE evolved fully as a mechanism for technology transfer. The second qualification is that the modern 'human skills endowments' variant of the HO theory must be used to explain trade patterns.

Although it can be argued that the simple theory works quite well it is evident that there are many important issues which it assumes away. Particular mention may be made of (i) economies of scale and transport costs, (ii) taxes and tariffs, and (iii) non-discriminating monopoly and monopsony.

Limited progress can already be made by applying geographical location theory, tax and tariff theory and the theory of imperfect competition to modify or replace the HO theory. However an integrated solution of these problems must await further developments in orthodox trade theory.

Policy

5 A policy for foreign direct investment

5.1 INTRODUCTION

This chapter is concerned with appraising the costs and benefits of FDI. Unlike previous studies[1] it does not focus on the role of capital flows, which we have argued are an incidental part of FDI. Instead it considers FDI as a consequence of the internalisation of markets for proprietary information and other intermediate products. The costs and benefits we consider are those of an internal market, in comparison to an external market.

In making such an appraisal it is important to distinguish between *private* and *social* costs and benefits. Private costs and benefits are those perceived by the firm, while social costs and benefits include effects which impinge on any member of society. In general terms, a social cost is anything which reduces world economic welfare, a social benefit is anything which increases it.

We shall attempt to establish the following propositions:

(i) The social costs of internalisation tend to be greater than the private costs;

(ii) The social benefits of internalisation are unnecessarily high because existing external market institutions are inadequate;

(iii) Some of the most widely condemned business practices of MNEs are socially as well as privately beneficial.

Our conclusion from (i) and (ii) is that on grounds of social efficiency there is at present too much FDI and too little 'arm's length' trade, and in particular too little licensing. Policies for achieving a socially efficient amount of FDI are discussed, and it is argued that 'first-best' policies can normally be implemented. However these policies may involve substantial changes in the systems of property rights in source and host countries. Our conclusion from (iii) is that there are some restrictive business

83

practices whose elimination would do nothing to improve efficiency, and would probably reduce it. Criticism of these practices merely diverts attention from more significant issues.

5.2　A COMPARISON OF PRIVATE AND SOCIAL COSTS

The private costs and benefits of internalisation were considered in Chapter 3. There appear to be at least three cases in which social costs and benefits differ significantly from private ones.

Firstly, the private benefit from transfer pricing normally exceeds the social benefit. This is because the minimisation of tax and tariff payments redistributes income from the public to the private sector. Such redistribution yields a private benefit but no corresponding social benefit. Also the change in effective rates of taxes and tariffs may reallocate resources. In so far as existing taxes and tariffs are optimal – either in eliminating externalities or in raising a given public revenue with minimal distortion – avoidance of them will impair social efficiency. Only if the taxes and tariffs are too high can transfer pricing lead to social gains. Subject to this qualification, it can be said that transfer pricing represents at best a redistribution of income which is socially neutral, and at worst the undermining of an optimal system of taxation and tariffs, which is socially damaging.

Secondly, the net private cost of market fragmentation may understate the true social cost, because fragmentation creates a barrier to entry which yields offsetting private gains and increased social losses.

Market fragmentation occurs when an internal market is closed: none of the commodity is either bought from or sold to outsiders. Closing a market reduced the firm's flexibility, and makes it difficult to operate each division at an optimal scale (see section 3.7). But there may be offsetting gains to the firm if closing the market creates a barrier to entry. When potential entrants to an industry are of unproven ability in that industry (as they almost inevitably are), they will normally be faced with a cost of capital which increases significantly with the amount to be borrowed; it is therefore much more costly to enter on a large scale than a small scale. If an established firm operates a closed internal market it can deny potential entrants to the supplying activity a market for their product and also deny entrants to the purchasing activity a source of supply. This obliges a potential entrant in either activity to enter as an integrated firm, and therefore increases the scale at which he must enter. This raises potential entrants' costs of capital and thereby establishes a barrier to entry which enhances the established firm's monopoly power in final product markets and its monopsony power in factor markets. There is no social gain, because the established firm's additional profit is exactly compensated by consumers' and factor owners' losses. There will be overall social loss if the established firms restrict output to maximise profit – the usual tactic in the absence of competition.

Finally, the private costs arising from the diversity of the firm's operations may understate the social costs. For a foreign investor a major problem of diverse foreign operations is acquiring information about his host environment. Failure to acclimatise quickly to the environment results in mistakes which impose costs not only on the firm but on host country interests – the government, native personnel deprived of training, etc. In many cases the injured parties cannot claim compensation from the firm. To the extent that the firm does not bear all the costs imposed by its mistakes, the private costs of diversity understate the social costs.

In each of the cases considered above, the net social benefit from internalisation is less than the corresponding private benefit. It follows that the degree of internalisation sought by profit maximising firms probably exceeds the degree of internalisation compatible with social efficiency. This suggests that the amount of FDI at present undertaken is probably excessive.

5.3 HARMONISING PRIVATE AND SOCIAL COST

Given that the private pursuit of maximum profit may lead to more internalisation than is socially desirable, the question naturally arises as to how to correct this.

It is convenient to distinguish three types of policy. The first attacks the root cause of the divergence between private and social cost by attempting to eliminate the cause of the discrepancy; this is the 'first-best' solution. The second type of policy does not attempt to remove the root cause, but rather to compensate for it by levying taxes or subsidies so that the private perception of relative costs of internal and external markets is the same as the social perception of relative costs. In this case the profit-maximising strategy for the private individual or firm is compatible with social efficiency, given that the original discrepancy cannot be removed. The third type of policy is similar to the second, but seeks to achieve social efficiency by constraining profit-maximising behaviour through quotas, prohibitions and other forms of non-price regulation.

There is little doubt that on grounds of administrative convenience the third policy is the most attractive. It avoids all the difficulties associated with removing the original discrepancy, and also avoids the problems associated with accounting and budgeting for taxes and subsidies. In practice this form of regulation of FDI has been the one most widely canvassed and most frequently implemented. However it is our contention that in the long run it is feasible to implement first-best policies, and that these policies are superior to both taxation/subsidisation and regulation.

The next three sections develop detailed proposals for correcting the discrepancies noted in section 5.2.

5.4   CLOSING LOOPHOLES THAT PERMIT TRANSFER PRICING

There are two first-best solutions to the problem of transfer pricing. The first is for governments to eliminate the incentive to manipulate prices by levying taxes and tariffs on a lump-sum rather than *ad valorem* basis; if payment is no longer related to value the manipulation of prices can no longer influence liability. However this would represent a very radical change – certainly in the case of taxation. A simpler solution is to tighten up existing legislation by establishing regulations for the pricing of internal transactions. Hitherto the enforcement of tax and tariff laws has focused on the detection of concealed transactions rather than on checking the economic soundness of reported prices. By establishing formulae for internal prices and requiring the auditing of prices it would be possible – at least in principle – to control manipulation. [2]

In practice it would be fairly straightforward to constrain prices to no less than average variable cost. In some cases it would also be possible to ascertain how much outside suppliers would charge for similar products or services and to set this as a ceiling on price. But within these limits the crucial question would concern what proportion of fixed costs should be allocated to the commodity. It is this question which has been at the root of most host country–MNE disputes over transfer prices. Now it is a well established proposition that the allocation of fixed costs is irrelevant to marginal decisions within the divisions of a firm. There is thus no reason why regulations governing the allocation of overheads should not be determined on an *ad hoc* basis; for example each division of the firm could be allocated overheads in direct proportion to its variable costs. Provided such regulations were rigidly enforced the internaliser will on balance neither gain nor lose with respect to tax and tariff liability, and the decision to internalise will be neutral with respect to the tax and tariff systems. These same regulations will also inhibit the internaliser from bypassing exchange control regulations.

5.5 REMOVING BARRIERS TO ENTRY THAT STEM FROM VERTICAL INTEGRATION

Two conditions are necessary for vertical integration to constitute a barrier to entry. Firstly, the internal market for the intermediate product must be closed, so as to deny potential competitors at one stage a source of supply or demand for their product. Secondly the management of a potential competitor must be faced with a rate of return which falls as the scale of entry increases.

The first condition refers to a restrictive practice which will tend to diminish social efficiency. It is therefore a legitimate object of competition policy to insist that internal markets be open. But in practice this objective may be difficult to achieve. It is evident that if the firm were to set a very low buying price and a very high selling price for the intermediate product then transactions with other firms would be effectively discouraged. It is therefore necessary to insist that buying and selling prices cannot differ by more than an amount which reflects the additional contractual cost incurred by transacting with an outside party. Subject to this restriction the firm may choose its own prices. The firm would then be obliged to set equilibrium prices. For if the average price were fixed too low it would be obliged to sell the intermediate product at an effective subsidy to competitors operating the final stage of production, while if it were fixed too high it would be obliged to buy at a premium from competitors operating the initial stage of production. If in addition governments insisted that internal prices were related to the prices offered to outsiders, the opportunities for transfer pricing would be effectively eliminated. Thus it appears that two problems can be resolved with a single policy.

There is however a difficulty with intermediate products produced under increasing returns to scale, for here pricing should either be discriminatory, or based on marginal cost with losses compensated by subsidy. Under such circumstances efficient regulation of the intermediate product market is difficult whatever type of administrative control is used.

The rate of return may diminish with the scale of entry for a number of reasons; we consider here just one possibility – that of an increasing cost of capital. One reason why the cost of capital rises is that not everyone has perfect information about the specific managerial abilities of a potential entrant. Those who do have perfect information may be willing to lend all they can at a given rate of interest, but as the scale of the required investment increases less well-informed sources will have to be tapped for finance. Since they perceive the risks to be higher they will require to be compensated by a higher rate of interest; the same will be true if the well-informed investors attempt to refinance themselves from the less well-informed. The problem rests ultimately on the difficulty of diffusing information within the capital market, difficulties which stem in part from shortcomings in the legal system. Firstly the risk of default faced by a potential lender will make him sceptical of any information presented to him on behalf of the borrower, while the risk of imitation or pre-emption by a potential lender will make the borrower wary of diffusing information about his planned investment. Changes in the law of bankruptcy and limited liability on the one hand, and an extension of the patent system on the other hand, would contribute toward eliminating these risks and encouraging the free flow of information in the capital market.

5.6   IMPROVING PERFORMANCE IN THE HOST ENVIRONMENT

The final discrepancy distinguished in section 5.2 arises because the foreign direct investor does not bear the full cost of his mistakes. This encourages the firm to underinvest in information about the host environment in the first place. This is the only case in which a first-best policy is not normally feasible. It would involve the firm's appropriating all the benefits from efficient decision-taking, instead of sharing them with other transactors, as usually happens in competitive markets. This is a special case of a general problem in the economics of information; it arises because the indivisibility of information makes it difficult for transactors to share out the provision of market information.

Several second-best policies are feasible:

(a) to subsidise the diffusion of relevant information to the firm;

(b) to tax its mistakes, i.e. to impose fines for particular types of anti-social behaviour, and

(c) to regulate the firm by requiring its actions to be vetted by a government body.

Each of these policies encourages the firm to invest more resources in the acquisition of information. But policies (b) and (c) increase the complexity of the institutional environment, hence increasing the need for information as well as encouraging the acquisition of it. The administrative costs of (b) and (c) are also likely to exceed those of (a). On these grounds a policy of subsidising the provision of information is to be recommended. The only disadvantage from the host country point of view is that the government redistributes income to the foreign investor; however this income can always be recouped through taxation.

5.7 IMPROVING PROPERTY RIGHTS IN EXTERNAL MARKETS

In Chapter 3 considerable emphasis was placed on external market imperfections connected with inadequate property rights and the costs of enforcing contracts. Given the existence of such imperfections, the private gain to the firm from bypassing these imperfections through internalisation also constitutes a social gain. But it is not at all obvious that the firm's solution of the problem is the best that can be achieved. Essentially the firm is creating well-defined internal rights backed up by effective internal sanctions to substitute for ill-defined external rights backed by ineffective or costly external sanctions. If a firm can create well-defined and enforceable property rights, it may be asked why society cannot do so too. It could be argued that society should be able to improve on the system used by the firm. If this is accepted, it follows that existing institutional arrangements in external markets should not be taken as a datum. There may exist superior institutional arrangements which, if implemented, would provide a better system of property rights than those internal to the firm, and thereby render the social benefit to internalisation negative. If access to this improved system of property rights were freely available to firms, the private benefit to internalisation would also become negative. Thus an improvement of external property rights would lead to the spontaneous 'dis-integration' of the operations of profit-maximising firms.

Three main problems with the law of property and contract may be distinguished: (a) the absence of clear economic thinking in formulating the objectives of the law, (b) the existence of 'loopholes', so that the law as actually drafted fails to achieve its objective, and (c) the costs of judicial procedures.

The absence of clear economic thinking is the main cause of excessive costs in external markets. This is very evident in the case of the two costs most relevant to the foreign direct investor, namely the costs of protecting proprietary interest in information and the cost of enforcing long-term futures contracts in intermediate products. We consider each of these costs in turn.

The patent system constitutes the legal basis for proprietary interest in information. The system operated today in most developed countries was designed to protect the small inventor against the predatory activities of the large organised innovator; it was never designed to protect the wide variety of proprietary information generated by the large-scale R and D programmes of the organised innovator himself. The reform of the patent system is a complex matter, and discussion of it is deferred till section 6.2. Suffice it to say that the present patent system is inadequate on a number of grounds, and that relatively straightforward modifications of the system would significantly reduce the contractual costs of technology transfer.

The enforcement of long-term futures contracts is made difficult by the legal right of parties to default in certain circumstances. An obvious example is the protection afforded by declaration of bankruptcy, and more generally by limited liability. A less obvious example is the protection afforded by labour laws for employees who renegue on long-term contracts of employment. The consequences of the latter can be very severe, for in industries where labour contributes a significant proportion of the value added, firms will be unwilling to enter long-term contracts for the supply of output unless they can insure themselves by long-term contracts for the supply of labour input. Thus even if demanders of the output were willing to tolerate the risk of supplier's default, the supplier may be unwilling to sell forward because of his exposure to risk in the labour market. These problems are avoided by internalisation because the distribution of income between supplier and demander no longer matters; only their combined income is important.

Changes in the law on bankruptcy, limited liability and employee protection would probably be more controversial than changes in patent law because they are of immediate importance to a much wider section of the community, and in the absence of a compensating extension of social security payments such changes could be construed as damaging the interests of less able individuals. For this reason we shall not attempt to evaluate such reforms in this book.

5.8 RESTRICTIVE BUSINESS PRACTICES WHICH ARE COMPATIBLE WITH EFFICIENCY

In section 1.7 it was noted that FDI is often accompanied by the use of restrictive business practices, in particular export restrictions on foreign subsidiaries and output-related royalties on technology transferred to foreign subsidiaries.

It is an implication of the analysis in Chapter 2 that such behaviour is characteristic of any efficient market mechanism for the transfer of proprietary technology. Such behaviour does not therefore constitute a case for the regulation of FDI. On the contrary, in so far as such behaviour promotes efficiency, policies should be designed to encourage it.

Consider first the use of export restrictions. Their main function is to help enforce price discrimination in international markets. The problem in enforcing price discrimination is to prevent arbitrage between high-price and low-price markets. Typically the high-price market is in a high-income developed country and the low-price market in a low-income LDC, although this may not apply if the inequality of personal incomes is much greater in the

LDC.[3] Now in theory tariffs may protect a high-price market from arbitrage originating in a low-price market. But in practice it tends to be high-income nations – where prices are high – which have the lowest tariffs, so that tariffs cannot usually be relied upon. Another possibility is that product differentiation may be used to orient tastes in high-income markets away from the product supplied to the low-income market. However the costs of differentiation are often high, and its success uncertain. By far the simplest way of preventing arbitrage is to regulate trade at the point of production, by restricting the exports of indigenous producers servicing the low-income markets. Provided such restrictions do not inhibit the servicing of markets from minimum-cost locations, the gains from the enforcement of price discrimination will not be offset by efficiency losses elsewhere. Thus by facilitating price discrimination, export restrictions can make a positive contribution to the development and diffusion of proprietary technology.

In some cases export restrictions cannot be enforced, either because of government policy or because violation of the restriction is difficult to detect. It may therefore be impossible to segment the world market, and so all licensees or foreign subsidiaries become potential competitors. We have previously established that the most efficient way of coordinating the output decisions of competing licensees is through an output-related royalty. This system of royalty is appropriate wherever there is substitutability between different uses (or different users) of the same proprietary information. Thus an output-related royalty, although it may be fairly described as a restrictive business practice, is nevertheless the most efficient royalty system in cases where market segmentation cannot be achieved. The same remark applies to equivalent systems, such as those involving the overpricing of a tied input, although these systems may be objectionable on other grounds (see section 6.4).

5.9 CONCLUSION

To achieve a socially efficient degree of internalisation governments should pursue three main policies. The first is to reform patent law to give additional protection to the licensor. The second is to 'open up' internal markets in intermediate products to give non-integrated competitors access to the market when they require it. The third – which is important mainly as an alternative to the second – is to introduce statutory formulae for the determination of internal prices in cases where no comparable external price exists.

A fourth policy – and one which is much more radical – would be to amend the laws of bankruptcy and limited liability, and the relevant parts of labour law to reduce the incentive to vertical integration. Implementation of this policy would obviate the need for the second policy, since if the law of contract were changed competitive pressures would tend to dis-integrate markets anyway.

If these policies were pursued it would be unnecessary to take further measures, such as taxation/subsidisation or non-price regulation, in order to achieve the optimal degree of internalisation. This is not to say, of course, that these further measures would not be required in other areas of a foreign direct investor's operations. Imperfections in the market for human capital may require the subsidisation of training, while distortions in domestic relative prices may require incentives for entry into certain sectors of business, the taxation of pollution-intensive activities, and so on. But none of these policies is directly relevant to the degree of internalisation.

6 The future contractual basis for technology transfer

6.1 INTRODUCTION

A major theme of this book is that there is considerable scope for substituting licensing for FDI. It is not claimed that licensing can be a perfect substitute for FDI, either now or in the foreseeable future. Rather there is a margin at which the costs and benefits of licensing versus FDI are equalised, and on social criteria this margin is more favourable to licensing than present practices would suggest.

The main factor inhibiting licensing is the inadequacy of the patent system. Section 6.2 considers the defects of the patent system, and presents practical proposals for its reform.

Section 6.3 places the discussion of licensing within the context of the debate on 'unbundling' the resources transferred to the host country by MNEs. A number of potential constraints on unbundling are isolated. Section 6.4 considers how some of these constraints can be avoided by subcontracting.

Section 6.5 considers the possibility of socialising all property in information. In the short run this would redistribute income from source to host countries; its long-term effect would depend on how the development of information was financed. It is argued that until socialisation takes place, control over the distribution of income will remain firmly in the hands of source countries.

The conclusions are summarised in section 6.6.

6.2 REFORM OF THE PATENT SYSTEM

The patent system, as organised in most developed countries, has three main shortcomings. Firstly its coverage is restricted mainly to technical information, whereas on efficiency grounds it should apply impartially to all information of significant economic value. Its limitations in the field of marketing information and managerial techniques are particularly noteworthy. Secondly it does not cover satisfactorily the re-use of information in subsequent research. An important use of any information is for investment in further development, which will eventually render the immediate application of the original information obsolete. Thirdly, the patent system fails to protect the originators of research programmes, thereby encouraging duplication or speeding up of research.

The first two limitations of the patent system encourage proprietors of information to maintain their exclusive access to information through secrecy. Now in principle it is possible to license a secret, although there are difficulties arising from buyer uncertainty. For example if individual X asks individual Y whether he wishes to pay to be let into a secret, Y will wish to know what the secret is before he pays. But once Y knows the secret information, there is no reason why he should pay X for what he already knows. Hence X will not tell Y what it is he is selling and therefore Y will be reluctant to buy. The maximum Y is willing to pay will be based on an expected value in which a positive probability attaches to the possibility that the information is worthless. [1] On the other hand X, having access to the information, has a valuation based on the certainty of what it is worth. The only way X can persuade Y to pay what he, X, knows the information to be worth is for X to insure Y against the possibility that the information is worthless. The insurance is costless to X, but serves to raise Y's valuation of the information to the certain valuation of X, so that contracting can now take place at this value. This form of insurance involves selling the information on a contingent contract.

However, there are considerable difficulties in monitoring and enforcing a contingent contract in which payment is related to the *ex post* value of the information. Because payment is made after the information has been transferred there is a relatively high risk of buyer's default, and because of the practical difficulties of valuing information it may be necessary to hire the services of an arbitrator. These costs encourage proprietors of information to abstain from licensing and exploit the information themselves through FDI.

Our analysis suggests that FDI will be prominent where the

information is of a marketing or managerial kind, since it is here that patent protection is weakest. It will also predominate in industries where items of information tend to be re-used in further research. Such industries will be characterised by a high rate of technical progress, and normally a high rate of obsolescence. Licensing will be disliked because of its tendency to 'build up' a competitor, and in extreme cases patenting may be avoided because the publicity may draw the attention of competitors to further uses of the patented information which the patentee would like to pre-empt for himself. Casual empiricism suggests that in the post-war period the pharmaceutical industry has been strongly influenced in this way. Once again, an extension of the patent system in this direction would encourage firms to license rather than exploit their information through FDI.

The third limitation of the patent system is seen in the behaviour of MNEs which is frequently diagnosed as 'oligopolistic': namely replication of short-term R and D projects, carried out 'against the clock' to avoid pre-emption by competitors. It can be argued that such behaviour is not a consequence of oligopoly – i.e. it does not follow immediately from the existence of a few leading firms; rather oligopoly is itself a consequence of lack of proper coordination of R and D projects, stemming from the lack of patent protection for research beginning or in progress. The same few firms are in continual competition to exploit new opportunities for research, the number of firms being determined by competitive forces so that at the industry level the potential profit – and hence the potential welfare gains – from the stream of information generated is exactly dissipated by the resource costs incurred through inefficiency in R and D.

The shortcomings of the patent system can be remedied by extending its coverage to all forms of information of significant economic value, giving the patentee protection against unlicensed improvements made using his information, and creating a patent right over research in progress. Although the main justification for these reforms is on grounds of efficiency, it may be noted that the changes would not necessarily redistribute income toward innovating firms, since they would make it possible for governments to charge firms for the use of the results of basic research. A detailed examination of the feasibility of these proposals is outside the scope of this book. However, we believe that the arguments in favour of them are sufficiently strong for the proposals to warrant serious consideration.

6.3 LIMITATIONS OF LICENSING

A conventional view of the MNE has been that it transfers a 'bundle' of resources to the host country. Debate has focused on the possibility of 'unbundling' this package.[2] We have already argued that MNEs' access to host capital markets enables them to separate the sourcing of capital from the sourcing of other transferable assets. Licensing may be perceived as a further step in unbundling the package. Indeed it is possible in principle to unbundle the whole of any package by licensing separately each element contained in it. But how far is it economic to pursue each unbundling?

Previous analysis (Chapter 3) has considered this issue in very general terms, but there are several specific points worth making as well. It is useful to distinguish four elements of the package potentially associated with FDI. They are (1) technical know-how, (2) marketing skill, (3) managerial skill and (4) supply of an intermediate product ready for processing. A fifth element – the supply of capital – is excluded from the discussion because the international capital market allows the provision of capital to be separated from the rest of the package whether or not the transfer is effected by FDI.

The case for 'unbundling' rests on the fact that different individuals and organisations have different comparative advantages in the supply of each of these resources. In a world of perfect markets the efficient strategy would be to obtain technical know-how from the source with the strongest comparative advantage in supplying know-how, to obtain marketing skills from the source with the strongest comparative advantage in marketing, and so on. It is by no means inevitable that the individual or organisation with a comparative advantage in technology also has a comparative advantage in marketing, in management and in the supply of intermediate products. For example it is unlikely that the efficient source of technology will have the local knowledge necessary to manage optimally the hiring of local labour and other factors of production.

However it is equally clear that there are dangers in separating the sourcing of certain elements. When marketing a product it is important to know what claims can be made for it, i.e. what qualities of the product can be legitimately advertised and guaranteed to the consumer. To frame such claims accurately it is necessary to be familiar with the technology of the product.

Where the technology is complex it may be efficient to unify the supply of technical know-how and marketing skills.

The design of high-technology equipment is often oriented to processing a specific type of intermediate product, so that machinery designed to process one type of material will not easily adapt to process other types. In such cases technology and intermediate product often originate from the same source. To commission alternative supplies of the intermediate product may involve a risk of technical incompatibility with the machinery. Thus when the quality of the intermediate product is a crucial factor it may be efficient to unify the supply of technical know-how and the supply of the intermediate product.

It is also true that high-technology equipment typically requires skilled labour to operate it. The nature of the skills required, and the appropriate method of screening for them, may be best understood by the developer of the technology. Thus when scarce skilled labour is a complementary input it may be efficient to unify the supply of technical know-how and the supply of managerial skills.

6.4 SUBCONTRACTING PRODUCTION, AND TIED INPUTS

Perhaps the most important constraint on 'unbundling' is the one arising from the need to unify the sourcing of technical and marketing skills: this appears to be significant in the pharmaceutical and computer industries, for example. Given the need to control both the development of the technology and the distribution of the product, licensing is out of the question and the only alternative to FDI is to subcontract production. Under subcontracting the day to day management of production is delegated to an indigenous firm; the technology is made available to the subcontractee, but all of his output using this technology is purchased by the subcontractor.

In principle subcontracting is quite an attractive alternative to licensing. In common with licensing it frees the proprietor of the technology from the management of production, which is the activity most dependent on knowledge of local conditions. But it avoids the licensor's problems of devising a royalty system for licensing to competing users and minimising buyer uncertainty.

The main drawbacks to subcontracting are that it may create a problem of quality control, and may eliminate gains from the vertical integration of production and marketing that a licensor might enjoy.

The constraint on unbundling arising from the need to unify the sourcing of technical know-how and intermediate products may suggest a justification for some of the tied input agreements which are common in technology transfer (section 1.7). However it does not explain why the purchases are made mandatory for the recipient of the technology. The element of compulsion suggests that the licensor envisages a situation in which it may be efficient for the licensee to use alternative sources. If this is the case then a tied input clause can only serve to reduce social efficiency. In practice tied inputs probably fulfil a dual role, in helping the licensor to monitor the licensee's operations and in concealing royalty payments as margins on overpriced inputs. Given that there exist other means of monitoring licensees' operations, it cannot be said that either of these roles contributes to social efficiency. Thus while there is good reason to believe that the proprietor of a technology may have a comparative advantage in the supply of complementary intermediate products, the use of tied input agreements to constrain the licensee's choice appears to be wholly objectionable on economic grounds.

The constraint on unbundling arising from the need to unify the sourcing of technical know-how and managerial skill strikes at the basis of licensing, since it implies that R and D and production should be under common control. If technical know-how and the relevant specific managerial skills are joint products of innovative activity there can be no satisfactory alternative to FDI. Unfortunately the extent to which they are joint products is difficult to judge from the available evidence. The only sure proposition is that the complementarity of technical and managerial skills is much greater in the early stages of a transfer, whilst the technology is still being adapted to its host environment. As adaptation takes place and operating skills diffuse within the working population managerial procedures become standardised and better suited for delegation. Thus even though FDI may be appropriate as a short-term expedient, it should be possible to 'spin-off' management in the long run and convert the contractual basis to licensing or subcontracting.

Our analysis suggests that limitations on 'unbundling' may

justify subcontracting and short-term investments as alternatives to licensing. However these limitations cannot justify tied input agreements. From the host country point of view it would appear that subcontracting and management spin-off agreements may be an acceptable basis for compromise when source-country interests are unwilling to license.

6.5 PRIVATE VERSUS PUBLIC INFORMATION: EFFICIENCY AND DISTRIBUTIONAL CONSIDERATIONS

In the preceding sections we have proposed an extension of the patent system. This proposal clearly conflicts with orthodox thinking on competitive policy, which regards patents as a barrier to entry, and therefore as a source of monopoly and inefficiency. To a certain extent orthodox thinking is influenced by the view that discriminatory pricing is not feasible, whereas our own view is that international price discrimination is a widely followed practice. The issue is significant because monopoly power distorts the allocation of resources only if uniform prices rather than discriminatory prices are used.

There is however a more fundamental difference, namely that orthodox policies aspire to the efficiency norm of atomistic competition with public access to information. This norm is largely incompatible with a situation where information is a 'produced good', since information, being diffusable, exhibits economies of scale in use, which makes atomistic competition in the development of information wasteful. Suppose however that the norm is waived with reference to the development of information, and is applied only to the use of information already developed. The orthodox policy is then to diffuse information at zero cost to everyone, so that all atomistic firms in an industry can compete on equal terms. If the information is privately developed then it is presumably sold to the state prior to intermediate use; alternatively the state may regulate the development of information and finance the process itself.

There are both pros and cons of diffusing information at zero cost. An advantage is that it avoids the costs of implementing price discrimination – in particular the costs of preventing arbitrage. Furthermore since the price is not merely uniform but also zero, it avoids all the costs of organising and policing the relevant contracts. A disadvantage is that when diffusing information at zero cost consumers do not reveal their valuation of the information through the price they are willing to pay, so that cost-benefit analysis of the development of information becomes a purely hypothetical exercise.

It is impossible to exclude considerations of equity from the issue of the ownership of information. An advantage of zero-cost diffusion of pubicly owned information is that the gains from the information accrue in the first instance to consumers, and the burden of the development cost is distributed among them through the tax system. This means that the administrative cost of maintaining an equitable distribution of income is fairly low. By contrast, with discriminatory pricing the whole of the surplus accrues in the first instance to the patentee, so that a large-scale redistribution of income is usually essential if equity is to be preserved. A disadvantage of zero cost diffusion is that it confers substantial powers on the state to determine the sort of information developed, either through the criteria applied to rewarding private developers or through direct control of which developments are to be undertaken.

It would seem that in the immediate future the world-wide socialisation of information is not politically feasible. In these circumstances the main dynamic of economic growth will continue to be proprietary information. The major issue facing host nations is, therefore, not whether information should be freely available, but how proprietary information can be used to greatest advantage. Efficiency criteria suggest that countries should host technologies in industries in which they have a comparative advantage. If a country believes that on the basis of relative factor costs it is the most competitive location for servicing a foreign market (e.g. in a developed country) it should negotiate to export to that market. It will have to pay – perhaps quite dearly – for such a right, but if it is indeed the least cost location then it will be able to outbid other parties for the right.

It may be objected on grounds of equity that with such a policy the whole of the quasi-rent associated with the new technology accrues to the source country. Now the quasi-rent in fact accrues to the entrepreneur who recognises the profit opportunity and not to the owners of skilled labour or risk-free (debenture) capital, whose services are purchased in competitive markets. In principle there is no reason why potential host countries should not act as entrepreneurs themselves, and hire source country labour and capital to generate technologies suitable to the host country environment. Alternatively they could subcontract development of the technology to source country firms. In either case the quasi-rent from the technology would accrue to the host country. Thus the international distribution of income from the use of technology is determined largely by the international distribution of entrepreneurial skill and not by the sources of labour and capital used in the development.

However, this result provides no comfort to countries whose endowments of entrepreneurship are small. Unless the terms of trade can be changed, such countries must continue to depend on aid. If donor countries wish to moderate the impact of the aid on their balance of payments, the aid could be tied in whole or in part to the purchase of the donor country's proprietary technologies. However, on grounds of efficiency donor countries should ensure that the burden of the aid does not fall disproportionately on the owners of proprietary information, since this will distort the allocation of resources away from the development of information, and impose a welfare loss on the world economy. Nevertheless the personal tax system in the donor country may be able to isolate the lifetime quasi-rent to pure entrepreneurial ability, in which case a tax on entrepreneurs can be imposed without any effect on the allocation of resources. An international redistribution of income in this way is unobjectionable on efficiency grounds.

We conclude that so long as information remains proprietary host country policies toward foreign investment cannot successfully redistribute income from the source country. The only initiative host countries can take is either to bargain for aid financed by source country taxation, or to take over the entrepreneurial function at present performed by the MNE. The latter strategy requires very scarce skills, and premature adoption of the strategy would simply result in mistaken decisions and very heavy losses. So long as the entrepreneurial function remains with developed countries, it is the developed countries' taxation policies which will determine the extent of income redistribution to LDCs.

6.6 SUMMARY: A SPECTRUM OF CONTRACTUAL ARRANGEMENTS

The increasingly critical attitude of host countries toward FDI is making it opportune to revitalise the concept of an international market for proprietary technology, where transfers of technology at present internal to firms are externalised by arm's length contracts between nationals of different countries.

It is already apparent that there is a trend toward much greater flexibility in the contractual basis for international technology transfer. There is much scope for promoting licensing, sub-contracting and management spin-off as alternatives to conventional FDI.

Host countries can promote 'market alternatives' to the MNE by offering legal safeguards to complement the patent system, e.g. by maintaining the confidentiality of marketing and managerial expertise transferred to them. Licensing of technology can be encouraged by offering the licensor the option of buying back production and marketing experience from the licensee at a fixed price.

It is unfortunate that when so many positive steps could be taken to promote these alternatives, UNCTAD and similar organisations are preoccupied with negative proposals for regulating and restricting the behaviour of MNEs. While such proposals may attract wide political support in the developing world, they represent at best a wasted opportunity for countries dependent on FDI.

Notes

1. STATEMENT OF THE ISSUES

1. Some writers exclude assets which are used solely in selling and distributing imported goods. For a classification of different types of MNE see R. D. Robinson, *International Business Management*, New York, 1973.
2. On the history and development of US-based MNEs see M. Wilkins, *The Emergence of the Multinational Enterprise*, Harvard, 1970 and *The Maturing of the Multinational Enterprise*, Harvard, 1974. For the British experience see R. D. Pearce, 'British investment in less developed countries – A general survey', *University of Reading Discussions Papers in International Investment and Business Studies*, No. 31, 1977, and J. M. Stopford, 'The origins of British-based multinational enterprises', *Business History Review* 48 (1974), pp. 303–35.
3. The post-war growth of US foreign direct investment was highlighted in J. J. Servan-Schreiber, *The American Challenge*, London, 1968, and analysed in C. P. Kindleberger, *American Business Abroad*, Yale, 1969. The counter-thrust by European firms in the US is described by R. Heller and N. Willatt, *The European Revenge*, London, 1975; see also L. Franko, *The European Multinationals*, London, 1976. The most recent phenomenon is the growth of Japanese investment overseas; see L. B. Krause and S. Sekiguchi, 'Japan and the world economy', in H. Patrick and H. Rosovsky (eds.), *Asia's New Giants*, Washington, 1976; K. Kojima, *Japan and a New World Economic Order*, London, 1977; M. Ikema, 'The Japanese investment abroad' (mimeo: Hitotsubashi University), 1977, and M. Y. Yoshino, *Japan's Multinational Enterprises*, Harvard, 1976.
4. The subject of MNE–host country relations has an enormous literature. Nearly 800 references are listed in M. Z. Brooke, M. Black and P. Neville, *A Bibliography of International*

Business, London, 1977. For an overview of the subject see R. J. Barnett and R. E. Muller, *Global Reach*, London, 1975, J. N. Behrman, *US International Business and Governments*, New York, 1971, R. Vernon, *Sovereignty at Bay*, London, 1971, and the same author's *The Economic and Political Consequences of Multinational Enterprise: An Anthology*, Harvard, 1972, and (with H. F. Johnson) *Storm over the Multinationals*, London, 1977. For a radical view of the impact of MNEs on LDCs see A. G. Frank, *Capitalism and Underdevelopment in Latin America*, New York, 1967, and O. Sunkel, 'Transnational capitalism and national disintegration in Latin America', *Social and Economic Studies*, Special Number 22 (1973), 135–70. For a critique of these views see R. Vernon, 'Multinational enterprises in developing countries: Issues in dependency and interdependence', in D. E. Apter and L. W. Goodman (eds.), *The Multinational Corporation and Social Change*, New York, 1976.

5. See G. D. A. MacDougall, 'The benefits and costs of private investment from abroad: A theoretical approach', *Economic Record*, 36 (1960), pp. 13–35, and M. C. Kemp, 'The benefits and costs of private investment from abroad: Comment', *Economic Record*, 38 (1962), 108–10, both reprinted in J. H. Dunning (ed.), *International Investment*, Harmondsworth, 1972.

6. See S. H. Hymer, *The International Operations of National Firms: A Study of Direct Investment*, Farnborough, 1976; also C. P. Kindleberger, *op. cit.*

7. The most influential definitions of LDCs are due to the World Bank, and are reviewed in M. McQueen, *Britain, the EEC and the Developing World*, London, 1977, Chapter 1.

8. The figures are for 1971; see United Nations, *Multinational Corporations in World Development*, New York, 1973, Table 27.

9. See OECD, *Stock of Private Direct Investment by DAC Countries in Developing Countries, End 1967*, Paris, 1972, Table 5, summarised in UN, *Multinational Corporations in World Development*, New York, 1973, Table 12. For more detailed information cf. J. W. Vaupel and J. P. Curhan, *The World's Multinational Enterprises*, Geneva, 1974, and T. Houston and J. H. Dunning, *UK Industry Abroad*, London, 1976.

10.　Cf. W. B. Reddaway, S. J. Potter and C. T. Taylor, *The Effects of UK Direct Investment Overseas: Final Report*, Cambridge, 1968. Nevertheless the experience of individual LDCs differs greatly. In some cases, such as the Bahamas and Bermuda, the book value of FDI is in excess of GNP; see G. L. Reuber et al., *Private Foreign Investment in Development*, Oxford, 1973.

11.　See the graphs presented by O. G. Whichard and J. N. Freidlin, 'US direct investment abroad in 1975'. *Survey of Current Business*, 56, No. 8, August 1976.

12.　For numerous examples of the domination of host country industries by direct investments sourced from particular countries see United Nations, *op. cit.*, Table 35. It is not only LDCs which experience this phenomenon; similar effects are observed with US investments in Canada, cf. A. E. Safarian, *Foreign Ownership of Canadian Industry*, Toronto, 1966.

13.　For a historical perspective on international capital flows see J. H. Dunning, 'Capital movements in the twentieth century', *Lloyds Bank Review*, April 1964, reprinted in J. H. Dunning, *Studies in International Investment*, London, 1970 and in J. H. Dunning (ed.), *International Investment*, Harmondsworth, 1972.

14.　Cf. United Nations, *op. cit.*, Table 42. This 'inflow–outflow' approach is extensively developed by S. Lall and P. Streeten, *Foreign Investment, Transnationals and Developing Countries*, London, 1977.

15.　See UNCTAD, *Major Issues arising from the Transfer of Technology to Developing Countries*, New York: United Nations, TD/B/AC. 11/10/Rev. 2, Table 13.

16.　See S. M. Robbins and R. B. Stobaugh, *Money in the Multinational Enterprise*, London, 1974.

17.　For classic statements of this view see C. Vaitsos, *Intercountry Income Distribution and Transnational Enterprises*, Oxford, 1974, and the same author's 'Bargaining and the distribution of returns in the purchase of technology by developing countries', *Bulletin of the Institute of Development Studies*, 3 (1970), pp. 16–23, reprinted in H. Bernstein (ed.), *Underdevelopment and Development*, Harmondsworth, 1976.

18.　It is argued in T. H. Moran, *Multinational Corporations and the Politics of Dependence*, Princeton, 1974, that bargaining power fluctuates over time. When the firm is about to expand, the host has very little bargaining power as it is interested in acquiring the technology. But, once the firm has invested, it is committed to the host and the balance begins to swing the other way. Overlaid on this pattern is a secular increase in host bargaining power as the host begins to develop skills which would enable it to run the subsidiary on its own without the parent firm.

2. THE CONCEPT OF EFFICIENCY AND ITS APPLICATION TO PROPRIETARY INFORMATION

1. This section provides a sketch of general equilibrium theory. For a fuller treatment see G. Debreu, *Theory of Value*, New Haven, 1959.

2. The analysis in this section relies heavily on the concept of consumers' surplus; cf. J. R. Hicks, *Value and Capital*, 2nd ed., Oxford, 1939. An alternative approach has been developed by G. W. McKenzie and I. F. Pearce, 'Exact measures of welfare and the cost of living', *Review of Economic Studies* 43 (1976), pp. 465–8. The use of price discrimination is discussed most extensively in the literature on public utility pricing; cf. R. A. and P. B. Musgrave, *Public Finance in Theory and Practice*, 2nd ed., New York, 1976, p. 696.

3. In other words, information is a 'public good'. The consequences for resource allocation are developed in K. J. Arrow, 'Economic welfare and the allocation of resources for invention', in National Bureau of Economic Research, *The Rate and Direction of Inventive Activity*, Princeton, 1962.

4. This aspect of the theory of patents is a special case of the theory of property rights in public goods. Cf. J. M. Buchanan, *Demand and Supply of Public Goods*, Chicago, 1968, and S. Cheung, 'The structure of a contract and the theory of a non-exclusive resource', *Journal of Law and Economics*, 13 (1970), pp. 49–70. The literature on patents is mainly of an applied nature, and does not offer much insight into the structure of an optimal patent system; a review of issues may be found in A. Silberston, 'The patent system', *Lloyds Bank Review*, 84 (1967), pp. 32–44, reprinted in D. M. Lamberton

(ed.), *Economics of Information and Knowledge*, Harmondsworth, 1976.
5. For earlier analyses along these lines see D. J. Teece, *The Multinational Corporation and the Resource Cost of International Technology Transfer*, Cambridge, Mass., 1976, and E. Mansfield, et al., *Research and Innovation in the Modern Corporation*, New York, 1971. For a general theory of the optimal timing of development see M. C. Casson, 'The time profile of production', *University of Reading Department of Economics, Discussion Papers*, No. 42, 1974.
6. This result needs to be applied with caution because in practice the replication of research effort is sometimes more apparent than real. Firstly, when information is being developed for commercial purposes, different researchers may have different applications in mind, so that research programmes are differentiated by objective. Secondly, because information is often developed under uncertainty about the appropriate research methodology, research programmes may be differentiated by strategy. Differentiation of research, whether by objective or by strategy, is compatible with efficiency, so that any patent on a research programme would have to be restricted to the achievement of a given objective by a given strategy.

3. THE RATIONALE OF THE MULTINATIONAL ENTERPRISE

1. The analysis in this chapter is an extension of the theory presented in P. J. Buckley and M. C. Casson, *The Future of the Multinational Enterprise*, London, 1976. The seminal work is R. H. Coase, 'The nature of the firm', *Economica N. S.*, 4 (1937), pp. 386–405. Other influential writings include A. A. Alchian and H. Demsetz, 'Production, information costs and economic organisation', *American Economic Review*, 62 (1972), 777–95; K. J. Arrow, 'The organisation of economic activity', in 'The analysis and evaluation of public expenditure: The PPB system', *Joint Economic Committee*, 91st Congress, 1st Session, 1969, pp. 59–75; K. J. Arrow, 'Vertical integration and communication', *Bell*

Journal of Economics, 5 (1975), pp. 173–83; B. J. Loasby, *Choice, Complexity and Ignorance*, Cambridge, 1975; H. Malmgren, 'Information, expectations and the theory of the firm', *Quarterly Journal of Economics*, 75 (1961), pp. 399–421; J. C. McManus, 'The theory of the multinational firm', in G. Paquet (ed.), *The Multinational Firm and the Nation State*, Toronto, 1972; E. T. Penrose, *The Theory of the Growth of the Firm*, Oxford, 1959; G. B. Richardson, *Information and Investment*, London, 1960; E. A. G. Robinson, *The Structure of Competitive Industry*, London, 1932; F. M. Scherer et al., *The Economics of Multi-Plant Operation*, Harvard, 1975, G. J. Stigler, *The Organisation of Industry*, Homewood, Illinois, 1968, and O. E. Williamson, *Markets and Heirarchies*, New York, 1975.

For a review of alternative theories of the MNE see J. H. Dunning, 'The determinants of international production', *Oxford Economic Papers*, 25 (1973), pp. 289–336, and the same author's 'Trade, location of economic activity and the MNE: A search for an eclectic approach', in B. Ohlin, P-O. Hesselborn and P. M. Wijkman (eds.), *The International Allocation of Economic Activity*, London, 1977. Interesting approaches to the theory of the MNE have been developed in A. Erdilek, 'Can the multinational corporation be incorporated into the general equilibrium theory of international trade and investment?' presented at the Western Economic Association, Las Vegas, 1974; T. Horst, 'Theory of the multinational firm', *Journal of Political Economy*, 79 (1971), pp. 1059–72; T. Horst, 'The theory of the firm', in J. H. Dunning (ed.), *Economic Analysis and the Multinational Enterprise*, London, 1974, and S. P. Magee, 'Multinational corporations, industry technology cycle and development', *Journal of World Trade Law* 11 (1977), pp. 297–321.

2. Most of the literature on the subject of price versus non-price market-clearing is to be found in the theory of planning. See G. M. Heal, 'Planning without prices', *Review of Economic Studies*, 36 (1969), pp. 347–62, and J. M. Montias, *The Structure of Economic Systems*, New Haven, 1976. For a comparison of negotiations and arbitration see W. Hildenbrand and A. P. Kirman, *Introduction to Equilibrium Analysis*, Amsterdam, 1976. For a more detailed study of negotiations see I. Stahl, *Bargaining Theory*, Stockholm,

1972 and L. G. Telser, *Competition, Collusion and Game Theory*, London, 1971.

3. The 'free rider' problem is discussed in N. M. Singer, *Public Microeconomics*, Boston, 1972, Chapter 6.

4. Cf. S. N. S. Cheung, 'Transaction costs, risk aversion and the choice of contractual arrangements', *Journal of Law and Economics* 12 (1969), pp. 23–42; H. Demsetz, 'The exchange and enforcement of property rights', *Journal of Law and Economics* 7 (1964), pp. 11–26, and H. Demsetz, 'The cost of transacting', *Quarterly Journal of Economics* 82 (1968), pp. 33–53.

5. There is an extensive recent literature on property rights. For a general survey see E. G. Furubotn and S. Pejovich (eds.), *The Economics of Property Rights*, Cambridge, Mass., 1974, and in particular see S. Pejovich, 'Towards an economic theory of the creation and specification of property rights', *Review of Social Economy*, 1972, pp. 309–25.

6. These are examples of 'transfer pricing'; see L. V. Niekels, *Transfer Pricing in Multinational Firms*, Stockholm, 1976. The wider consequences of transfer pricing are examined in S. Lall, 'Transfer-pricing by multinational manufacturing firms', *Oxford Bulletin of Economics and Statistics*, 35 (1973), pp. 173–95, and D. Macaluso and R. G. Hawkins, 'The avoidance of restrictive monetary policies in host countries by multinational firms', *University of Reading Discussion Papers in International Investment and Business Studies*, No. 25, 1976.

7. The problem of monitoring the quality of managerial services arises from the conflict of interests between management and shareholders. It is extensively discussed in R. L. Marris, *The Economic Theory of Managerial Capitalism*, London, 1964 and O. E. Williamson, *The Economics of Discretionary Behaviour*, Englewood Cliffs, New Jersey, 1964.

4. A THEORY OF FOREIGN DIRECT INVESTMENT, TECHNOLOGY TRANSFER, TRADE AND CAPITAL MOVEMENTS

1. For attempts to incorporate intermediate products into the HO theory see R. E. McKinnon, 'Intermediate products and

differential tariffs: A generalisation of Lerners' symmetry theorem', *Quarterly Journal of Economics*, 80 (1966), pp. 584–615; J. R. Melvin, 'Intermediate goods, the production possibility curve and gains from trade', *Quarterly Journal of Economics*, 83 (1969), pp. 141–51, and R. D. Warne, 'Intermediate goods in international trade with variable proportions and two primary inputs', *Quarterly Journal of Economics*, 85 (1971), pp. 225–36.

2. It should be noted that if account is taken of the re-export from country 2 of the first-stage output embodied in the finished product then trade flows will be augmented in value by *US*; however the gross recorded flow *UR* will contain an element of double-counting.

3. Although technical progress has been extensively analysed in trade theory, very little has been written on proprietary technology. The most relevant writings are R. Findlay, 'Relative backwardness, direct foreign investment and the transfer of technology: A simple model', Institute for International Economic Studies, University of Stockholm, mimeo; S. Hirsch, 'An international trade and investment theory of the firm', *Oxford Economic Papers*, 28 (1976), pp. 258–70; H. G. Johnson, *Technology and Economic Interdependence*, London, 1975, and R. W. Klein, 'A dynamic theory of comparative advantage', *American Economic Review*, 63 (1973), pp. 173–84. There is also a substantial literature on the related subject of the product life-cycle; see in particular R. Vernon, 'International investment and international trade in the product cycle', *Quarterly Journal of Economics*, 80 (1966), pp. 190–207, the same author's 'Location of economic activity', in J. H. Dunning (ed.), *Economic Analysis and the Multinational Enterprise*, London, 1974; G. C. Hufbauer, 'The impact of national characteristics and technology on the commodity composition of trade in manufacturing goods', in R. Vernon (ed.), *The Technology Factor in International Trade*, New York, 1970, pp. 145–213, and L. T. Wells, Jr (ed.), *The Product Life Cycle and International Trade*, Harvard, 1972.

4. A Hicks-neutral technical improvement is one which leaves invariant the marginal rate of substitution at any given level of factor intensity.

5. Cf. D. R. Lessard, 'World, national and industry factors in

equity returns', *Journal of Finance* 29 (1974), pp. 379–91;
W. P. Lloyd, 'International portfolio diversification of real
assets: An inquiry', *Journal of Business Research*, 3 (1975),
pp. 113–20, and A. M. Rugman, 'Motives for foreign
investment: The market imperfections and risk diversification
hypotheses', *Journal of World Trade Law* 9 (1975), pp.
567–73.

6. On the connection between trade and capital movements see
R. W. Jones, 'International capital movements and the
theory of tariffs and trade', *Quarterly Journal of
Economics*, 81 (1967), pp. 1–38 and I. F. Pearce and D. C.
Rowan, 'A framework for research into the real effects of
international capital movements', in T. Bagiotti (ed.), *Essays
in Honour of Marco Fanno*, Padova, 1966, pp. 505–35,
reprinted in J. H. Dunning (ed.), *International Investment*,
Harmondsworth, 1972.

5. A POLICY FOR FOREIGN DIRECT INVESTMENT

1. Some methodological issues in appraising the costs and
benefits of FDI are considered in J. H. Dunning, 'Evaluating
the costs and benefits of foreign direct investment: Some
general observations', *University of Reading Department of
Economics Discussion Papers in International Investment and
Business Studies*, No. 32, 1977. For an appraisal of costs and
benefits see G. L. Reuber et al., *op. cit.*, Chapter 2, and
R. Murray, 'The internationalisation of capital and the
nation state', *New Left Review*, 67 (1971), pp. 84–109,
reprinted in H. Radice (ed.), *International Firms and Modern
Imperialism*, Harmondsworth, 1975.

2. Cf. J. N. Bhagwati (ed.), *Illegal Transactions in International
Trade: Theory and Measurement*, Amsterdam, 1974.

3. A typical industry is publishing. The case is not so clear-cut
in the pharmaceutical industry, where prices are sometimes
higher in LDCs than in developed countries. This may be
partly due to the greater risks of servicing LDC markets,
but most probably reflects the fact that in LDCs only the
richest people demand pharmaceuticals, and their demand is
relatively price inelastic.

6. THE FUTURE CONTRACTUAL BASIS FOR TECHNOLOGY TRANSFER

1. Vaitsos, *op. cit.*, has argued that buyer uncertainty may lead the buyer to pay too much for a product, because the buyer's ignorance weakens his bargaining power *vis-a-vis* the seller. This seems to be incorrect. According to the theory of competitive games, it is the buyer's knowledge, not of the product itself, but of alternative sources of supply of the product, or the availability of substitute products, which strengthens his bargaining power. Even though the buyer does not know what the product *is*, he may know what it *does*, and hence be able to evaluate alternatives. The only way in which ignorance of the product itself is disadvantageous is if the seller intends to practise deception, and the buyer is without suspicion. But once the buyer becomes suspicious, his valuation of the product will tend to become less, rather than more, than the seller's, as explained in the text. When the correct interpretation of buyer uncertainty is recognised, Vaitsos' policy conclusions are invalidated.

2. See for example P. Streeten, 'New approaches to private investment in less developed countries', in J. H. Dunning (ed.), *International Investment*, Harmondsworth, 1972.

Index